CRAIG HIGGINSON
THREE PLAYS

Craig Higginson

THREE PLAYS

Dream of the Dog
The Girl in the Yellow Dress
The Imagined Land

OBERON BOOKS
LONDON

WWW.OBERONBOOKS.COM

This collection first published in 2016 by Oberon Books Ltd
521 Caledonian Road, London N7 9RH
Tel: +44 (0) 20 7607 3637 / Fax: +44 (0) 20 7607 3629
e-mail: info@oberonbooks.com
www.oberonbooks.com

A catalogue record for this book is available from the British Library.

PB ISBN: 9781783197248
E ISBN: 9781783197354

Cover image by Craig Higginson

Printed and bound by CPI Group (UK) Ltd, Croydon, CR0 4YY. eBook conversion by Lapiz Digital Services, India.

Visit www.oberonbooks.com to read more about all our books and to buy them. You will also find features, author interviews and news of any author events, and you can sign up for e-newsletters so that you're always first to hear about our new releases.

CONTENTS

Acknowledgements

Craig Higginson would like to thank his agent Jessica Cooper and her assistant Kat Buckle at Curtis Brown, as well as everyone at Oberon Books, including James Hogan, George Spender, James Illman, Emma Hall, Tia Begum and Konstantinos Vasdekis. He would also like to thank the contributions of all the people involved in the development and production of these plays. Special thanks to my wife Leila Henriques and to Jeremy Herrin, Malcolm Purkey and Michael Titlestad.

Foreword

I first met Craig Higginson in 2006 when I spent some time working with young writers from the Market Theatre Laboratory, as part of a creative exchange with Live Theatre, Newcastle upon Tyne. Craig was the Market's Literary Manager and organised my sessions. The writers showed a desire to understand the state their country was in, and despite their ambitions to write the definitive play about the troubled journey from apartheid to constitutional democracy, their theatrical canvases were often too wide to achieve the desired impact. Craig booked himself in for a conversation about the play that eventually became *Dream of the Dog*, an ostensibly small play that in its nuanced precision tells a huge story.

A collaborative friendship was born. Over a few years of return visits, I got to know South Africa, and Craig was a generous cultural and geographical guide to this beguiling and terrifying land. His insight into South Africa was offered with intellectual rigour and laced with sly and absurd humour. His tone was suffused with the sort of fatalism that seemed a sensible way to cope with the inequality and violence that comes with living in the thin air of Johannesburg.

These virtues are the bedrock of this collection of plays; and this particular sample of work shows him at his miniaturist best. The canvas may not be broad, but the work goes deep. The pairing of delicate psychology and considered plot allow the plays to move beyond the realism of their settings into a bespoke theatrical landscape, a place where the contradictions and messiness of contemporary life hold themselves up for inspection. The questions within *Dream of the Dog* are specific to place, but *The Imagined Land* speaks more broadly of the space where national and personal amnesia meet, and how a personal need for definition asserts itself in the face of trauma. *The Girl in a Yellow Dress* takes Craig off South African soil, and targets his interrogations more specifically at language and Europe's need to avoid the challenging reality of post colonial Africa. But all three plays talk congruently about how competing narratives need to find a way to coexist. What better theme for contemporary South Africa?

Despite his bloodless ability to bear witness to reality, optimism is never too far away and Craig's is a robust, hard-won South African variety. It is clearly reflected in these plays. His characters invariably turn towards the light. They have an inclination for the truth, even if reconciliation might still be beyond them.

Jeremy Herrin
Artistic Director Headlong
London
February 2016

Introduction

From 1996, when the first hearings began, The Truth and Reconciliation Commission exerted a considerable – even definitive – influence on South African literature and theatre. The Commission was based on principles of restorative justice: victims were accorded a context in which to face perpetrators and these agents of the state would be exonerated only in exchange for full disclosure. This ecclesial logic – confession, expiation and forgiveness – proved to be more symbolic than real. Only a minority of victims and perpetrators appeared before the Commission and the proceedings became mired in opposing definitions of truth and contested memories. Yet the hearings went a considerable way to rectifying and supplementing the apartheid public record. Covert military operations, assassinations, detentions without trial and disinformation had left constitutive silences in our history and at least some of these were given voice.

It would be inaccurate to interpret *Dream of the Dog* (2007), *The Girl in the Yellow Dress* (2012) and *The Imagined Land* (2015) as programmatic engagements with the Truth and Reconciliation Commission. They are neither pedantically political nor do they endorse the instrumental version of testimony on which – given its remit – the Commission was forced to settle. Rather, the plays comprise a succession of enquiries into the complex relations between narrative and actuality, between memory and its erasure, and between authorized and occluded voices. Since they are not limited to a specific agenda (the impulse to present a singular truth, a semblance of healing and nation-building), the plays can address those questions that unsettled the Commission but which it prudently and strategically underplayed.

Dream of the Dog was one of the most auspicious debuts in contemporary South African theatre – culminating in a West End transfer to the Trafalgar Studios of the Finborough Theatre production, which featured Janet Suzman. The play is currently a prescribed text in several universities in South Africa, the UK and North America. It concerns four enmeshed lives: Richard and Patricia Wiley, an aging couple in the process of leaving their desultory farm in the Natal Midlands to live in Durban; Beauty, their long-suffering domestic worker; and, Looksmart (whose isiZulu name is Phiwayinkosi Ndlovu), a post-apartheid entrepreneur who grew up on the farm. Richard is suffering the steady encroachment of Alzheimer's disease. Characteristic of the illness, certain memories are vivid, while the chronology and details of others are becoming increasingly mangled. The repressed memory in which the climax of the play consists is the deadly attack by a dog on Grace, a young worker on the farm. Richard was paying her to have sex with him. Pregnant by him and intending to keep the child, Richard loosed the vicious dog in the knowledge that it might kill Grace.

Richard's amnesia presents the tenuous and unreliable nature of memory. There is no simple retrieval of the past and no easy moral restitution. Patricia and Looksmart are also implicated in the torsion of remembering. The interaction between them reveals – after she initially fails to recognize Looksmart – that Patricia sentimentalizes the details of her role in raising him. Looksmart recalls the past in a different register. For him, all childhood memories are occluded by the day of Grace's death. He believes that she died en route to the hospital because Patricia hesitated for fear of getting blood on the upholstery of her car. Beauty discloses another misapprehension under which Looksmart has laboured. Grace never loved him and had no intention of marrying him. The mildly vengeful conviction that has motivated his acquisition of the farm – with the intention of turning it into an affluent gated community – is based on slippage. Further, his intention to replicate the farmhouse in the design of the range of new homes is ambiguous. At one level it grasps the apartheid original and devalues it through its multiplication in simulacra. At another it stages the way in which, not only Looksmart, but all the characters are embedded in pasts they ineluctably replicate. There is no emotional or intellectual mechanism that allows them to fix the past in its place and, by so doing, institute a truly original future.

While *Dream of the Dog* was a remarkable debut, *The Girl in the Yellow Dress*, which has had a number of local and international runs and is also a prescribed university text, is perhaps Higginson's most celebrated play to date. Inspired by Ovid's *Echo and Narcissus*, it superficially eschews South African preoccupations. It renders a series of finely crafted dialogues between Celia, a trust-funded young English woman living in Paris who teaches English as a foreign language, and a French student, Pierre. Each session reveals more about the history of the characters, wittily combining the roles of teacher and student and the intricacies of English grammar to reflect on the ways in which we construct ourselves and one another in the languages we know and those we are endeavoring to learn.

It soon becomes evident that Pierre understands the cultural currency of the social dispositions embedded in the English language. Since seeing her putting up signs at the Sorbonne, Celia has become Pierre's aspirational ideal; he imagines that, by teaching him the English language (and manners), she can usher him into the fullness of a European identity. He also hopes for an intimate association with his particular alterity through becoming her lover. In order to win her over, he tells her about his history of harm. He was, he claims, brought to France as a child by Médecins Sans Frontières after a violent attack by Hutu *interahamwe* on his East Congolese village. It transpires, though, that this is not Pierre's but his mother's story. He tells it because he imagines it to be the narrative Celia wants to hear from him; a tale of trauma on 'the dark continent'. In fact, Pierre grew up in France; he is a second-generation immigrant who continues to feel yoked to his family's past and confined to the various roles he is expected to play as an African student at a French university.

Celia's entrapment is a consequence of an incestuous desire for her brother. This transgressive longing – which was possibly actualized in an affair – leaves her trapped in self-loathing and consequent loneliness. In an explosive consummation, each reaches out of their particular confinement. After this sexual intimacy, Pierre and Celia retreat into entrapment by their pasts. Yet *The Girl in the Yellow Dress* does not propose worlds adamantly sealed off from one another. The play concludes with a portrayal of a hesitant mutuality – once again expressed in the form of a grammar lesson. Despite lapsing into fixed subject positions, Celia and Pierre glimpse the prospect of an alternative; a reality in which individuals are not fixed by their historical, emotional and racial embedding.

The recognition of this prospect relates to South Africa in which whites and blacks have generally been proximate strangers. The restrictions which history has imposed on intersubjectivity have been inordinate and determinative. Higginson's vision tests this political and existential reality – at a Parisian remove – without unmitigated pessimism.

The Imagined Land returns to Johannesburg; to a situation in which a young black Zimbabwean academic, Edward, is writing the biography of an aging (originally Rhodesian/ Zimbabwean) writer, Bronwyn, at the same time as he interacts with her daughter, Emily, rekindling an intimate relationship. Reminding us of Richard in *Dream of the Dog*, Bronwyn – in this instance as a consequence of brain surgery – is losing her memory. The narrative of her life is unraveling at the same time as her biographer seeks to mine it for keys, particularly the origin of Bronwyn's strained relationship with Emily. Edward conjectures – in his view, deduces – that Bronwyn left her child unprotected from the advances of a black consciousness poet; that, in short, she chose her literary career and her need for political validation over Emily's safety and well-being. As a politicized aesthete, Edward believes, Bronwyn was prepared to sacrifice anything to address her obsession with white complicity and guilt. Parallel to Edward's self-serving archaeology, Emily reconstructs subtler realities about her family's Zimbabwean past: intimacies and betrayals from which their lives were fashioned. Existence, it transpires, cannot be reduced to singular determining moments, rather it is a filigree; a composite, intricate pattern of linked representations. 'Research', in the sense that appeals to Emily, is a process of (repeatedly) looking again for patterns and possibilities; anything else is simply expedient ideology.

The play concludes with Edward having been appointed as a lecturer in the English department at a preeminent Johannesburg university, while Emily, who applied for the same job, plans to leave South Africa to take up a position at a university in Perth, Australia. But Edward's reduction of Bronwyn's life, his expedient scripting of her art and politics, is not conclusive. In a final conversation, Emily tries to expose Edward's motives for imposing his own narrative onto Bronwyn's life. In a political act, Edward initially withholds an explanation, yet when he learns about the miscarriage of his and Emily's child, a new space for mourning and exchange is opened. The play implies that Emily will hear his story only after the play has concluded. Here Higginson is suggesting that the 'traumatic' black narrative – which is so often represented in plays intended for predominantly white audiences, both inside and outside of South Africa – will be made available for Emily while still remaining generally unavailable.

We can conclude somewhat hesitantly that the three plays in this volume comprise an arc. While *Dream of the Dog* presents an almost impossible quest for the past, *The Girl in the Yellow Dress* opens the way to a constructive mutuality, although it withholds any definitive actualization. *The Imagined Land* is unapologetic about representing contemporary South Africa as propelled by a rudimentary politics of redress which overlooks the subtleties of the intersection of the personal and the political. We progress, in other words, from allegory to realism. Yet it is the plays' common concern with the possibilities and limits of representation – particularly with the emergence and strengthening of black South Africans' voices – that gives them unity. Collectively they refract what has been at stake in this country's transition, and they do so with a subtlety and insight that will ensure their longevity.

Michael Titlestad
University of the Witwatersrand

DREAM OF THE DOG

Production History

Dream of the Dog first appeared as a radio play on SAFM in South Africa in 2006, directed by Craig Higginson. It was rewritten as a stage play and premiered at the National Arts Festival (NAF) on 2 July 2007, produced by the NAF and the Market Theatre, before transferring to the Market Theatre. In 2008, it was revised and played at the Hilton Arts Festival. On 27 April 2010, a further revised version opened at the Finborough Theatre, London, produced by Meeting Point Productions. Shortly afterwards, that production transferred to the Trafalgar Studios.

In 2015, Craig Higginson published a novel called *The Dream House* (Picador Africa), which was inspired by this play. It appeared in French in 2016 as *Maison de rêve* (Mercure de France).

The current published text should be considered the final and definitive version of the play.

For the Market Theatre production:

Cast

PATRICIA	Vanessa Cooke
RICHARD	Peter Terry
BEAUTY	Given Lunga
LOOKSMART	Mncedisi Shabangu

Production Team

Director	Malcolm Purkey
Assistant Director	James Albrecht
Designer	Sasha Ehlers
Lighting	Nomvula Molepo
Producer	Regina Sebright

For the Finborough Theatre production:

Cast

PATRICIA	Janet Suzman
RICHARD	Bernard Kay
BEAUTY	Gracy Goldman
LOOKSMART	Ariyon Bakare

Production Team

Director	Katie McAleese
Designer	Alex Marker
Lighting	Michael Nabarro
Sound	Andrew Pontzen
Costumes	Penn O'Gara
Producer	Libby Brodie

Characters

PATRICIA

RICHARD

BEAUTY

LOOKSMART

The action takes place in real time, several years after the new millennium, in KwaZulu-Natal, South Africa. Dialogue in Zulu is in italics, followed by a translation in brackets.

The sitting room of the Wiley's farmhouse in the KwaZulu-Natal Midlands. It is late afternoon, early summer. Outside, there is a thick mist. There are piles of boxes and framed pictures stacked against the walls. Pale rectangles on the walls mark the places where the pictures once hung. Old rosettes from horse shows, riding hats, yellowing documents and bits of fishing equipment fill the boxes. There is an armchair and a table, on which lie a plate of apples and a knife, with a standard lamp alongside it. A mantelpiece testifies to a rather grander past. A faded Persian rug and some animal skins are scattered across the floor. Yellow flystrips, covered in dead flies, hang from the ceiling.

PATRICIA is looking through one of the boxes, deciding what to keep and what to discard. She may have a black rubbish bag for the things she wants to throw away. When she moves, she does so with some difficulty.

PATRICIA: Richard? Have you gone yet? Richard! Are you there? What the hell's he up to?

She pages through an old magazine and then digs up a framed picture of a young man on a motorbike. Her face glows quietly with some pleasing recollection.

PATRICIA: Richard!

RICHARD enters holding a pair of boots and a spade.

RICHARD: Who told you to buy new furniture?

PATRICIA: Does this look like new furniture?

RICHARD: I'm not sure I like those animal skins lying about.

PATRICIA: Then you shouldn't have shot the animals.

RICHARD: I shot those?

RICHARD regards them sceptically.

PATRICIA: Have you taken your pills?

RICHARD: Of course I've taken my pills.

He is about to sit on one of the boxes.

PATRICIA: Careful!

RICHARD: Of what?

PATRICIA: I'm tired of you breaking things. That's what. *(Gesturing to another box.)* Sit there. That's rosettes.

Instead of sitting, RICHARD wanders over to PATRICIA's armchair. He picks up the apple and the knife and cuts off a piece of apple.

RICHARD: You want?

PATRICIA: What are you planning to do with that spade?

RICHARD: I keep seeing her. All broken up. Lost in a heap of rubble.

PATRICIA: We've gone over this, Richard. I made it very clear in the agreement. The site will be protected.

RICHARD: Where's the television gone?

PATRICIA: Packed.

RICHARD: Someone must've taken it.

PATRICIA: Beauty packed it.

RICHARD: What for?

PATRICIA: We're leaving. Tomorrow. Everything has to be packed.

RICHARD: Leaving? *(He looks at the boxes.)* Then I want to take the dog.

PATRICIA: Of course we're taking the dog.

RICHARD: To my father's place. I want to take him there tonight.

PATRICIA: That's impossible.

He stares at her.

PATRICIA: Your father died twenty years ago.

RICHARD: That's extremely unlikely.

PATRICIA: Too many pies.

Silence.

PATRICIA: Don't you remember how you dithered about the funeral? You said if you went back to England, you may never come back. Imagining, I suppose, that everyone would find it a great loss.

RICHARD: But I saw him yesterday. We shared a cigarette. You think I was addressing his ghost?

He sits on the box with rosettes and starts to put on his boots.

PATRICIA: I think it will rain. I don't advise going out. The last time you went, you disappeared for the whole night. Bheki eventually found you up in top woods. Fast asleep inside a porcupine hole you'd scooped out.

RICHARD grunts.

PATRICIA: You looked hilarious, I might add. Half dressed. Twigs in your hair. Starlings nesting in your beard. And what did you achieve in the end? Bronchitis for a month.

RICHARD: Who are we talking about?

PATRICIA: You.

RICHARD: You know I don't like that.

PATRICIA: What else would you like to talk about?

RICHARD is still struggling with his boots.

RICHARD: I was dreaming. Before I came here.

PATRICIA: I could hear you snoring.

RICHARD: I was dreaming that we were dead.

PATRICIA nods – as if she's heard all this before.

RICHARD: We were in Heaven or Hell. I wasn't sure which. I don't think it mattered. All that mattered was that we were dead and we didn't know it. No one had decided to mention it.

PATRICIA: Who would have mentioned it?

RICHARD: God could have. Or one of his angels.

PATRICIA: Well you can relax. Because we're not.

RICHARD: We're not?

PATRICIA: Not quite.

He tries again with his boots.

RICHARD: Because it's coming.

PATRICIA: What is coming?

RICHARD: The ambulance. I said I have two dead children for you to pick up.

PATRICIA: What do you mean two?

RICHARD: You know what?

PATRICIA: No.

RICHARD: You think I'm not here, but I am.

PATRICIA: Roo – I know very well you're here.

Silence.

RICHARD: When I was three, my whole family went away.

PATRICIA: It was only your mother who went away.

RICHARD: No, I don't think that's right.

RICHARD makes to get up.

PATRICIA: Richard, I want you to concentrate. If you have to go out. For a walk. Some air. For the sake of generally plodding about – you can. Alright? But go to the stables. Get Bheki. Tell him to come with.

RICHARD: Alright.

He moves towards the spade.

PATRICIA: You don't need that spade. You're to walk around the stables a few times with Bheki and then come straight back. Is that understood?

RICHARD: Absolutely.

Silence.

RICHARD: Understood absolutely.

He moves away from the spade, looking defeated.

RICHARD: When I'm gone are you at least going to tidy up? It's impossible to find anything in this place.

PATRICIA: What have you lost?

RICHARD: It's not always clear. I get confused. Everything's such a bloody mess.

PATRICIA: Tell me about it.

RICHARD: Why did you bring us here? What did you expect? There's nothing out there. Not a soul to talk to. I stood at the end of the dirt road. It went as far as my eyes could look. But there was nothing at the end of it. Just another hill. Who would live to hell and gone like this?

PATRICIA: Us.

Silence.

PATRICIA: Tomorrow, Roo, we're going to the sea. We went once on your motorbike. You drove us all the way from the farm to Sheffield beach. You buried me in the sand, right up to my neck, and kissed me. There was sand in my mouth from laughing. We stayed up all night. And went for a swim as the sun was coming up. Just the sea and us, and the pale green haze of the hills beyond the shore. The sugarcane. In the mist. There was not a soul to disturb our peace. It was paradise. You were paradise. We both were.

RICHARD: That was another man.

PATRICIA: Too damn right.

RICHARD: At least I never married you.

PATRICIA: Actually – you did.

RICHARD: Well if I did, I did it to please you.

Silence.

RICHARD: Always getting what you want.

PATRICIA laughs with bitterness.

PATRICIA: Go on. Go for your bloody walk.

He leaves.

PATRICIA: And mind you don't fall down a donga and break your neck.

Silence.

RICHARD re-enters.

RICHARD: Outside there's a bloody fog. I can't see my hand in front of my face.

PATRICIA: It isn't fog, it's mist. Will you never learn?

RICHARD picks up the spade. PATRICIA moves towards him as fast as she can.

PATRICIA: Richard, I don't have time for this.

RICHARD: There are strange people in the shed.

PATRICIA: Give me that spade!

RICHARD leaves with the spade.

PATRICIA: Damnit. Richard! Beauty!

Silence.

PATRICIA: Beau-ty!

BEAUTY enters. She is a small woman, dressed in blue overalls, a doek on her head. Her feet are bare. She is neat, deferential, difficult to read. Whenever PATRICIA calls her, she does so in a song-like way, the second note much higher than the first.

PATRICIA: Richard has gone off again. With the spade.

BEAUTY: What must I do?

PATRICIA: Get him. Or get Bheki to get him.

BEAUTY: I will go, Mesis.

PATRICIA: *Ngiyabonga* (thank you).

Silence.

PATRICIA: And Beauty? Go to Rachel first. Then you can check on the stables and the chicken shed. You know what happens when he can't find the animals. He goes out to look for them. He tries to herd them back in from the hills.

BEAUTY: *Yebo* (Yes), Mesis.

From the front garden, a dog has started to bark.

PATRICIA: Mesis?

PATRICIA: It's probably the civet. Leave it.

BEAUTY peers through the window that overlooks the front garden and the stoep.

BEAUTY: I can see a silver car standing under the tree. *Angimboni umshayeli* (But I can't see the driver).

PATRICIA: Well it can't have driven there itself. Maybe the driver's gone around the back.

BEAUTY: Must I go and look?

PATRICIA: Yes – go look. And afterwards find Richard. I don't want him digging anything up.

BEAUTY: *Yebo*, Mesis.

With a quick habitual bob of the head, BEAUTY leaves.

The barking grows more ferocious.

The front door clicks closed.

Someone has arrived in the hallway, outside the sitting room, just out of sight.

PATRICIA: Hello? Beauty? Bea-uty!

Silence.

PATRICIA: Who is that?

Silence.

PATRICIA looks at the fruit knife. It is just out of reach.

PATRICIA: What do you want?

The shadowy presence remains at the doorway.

LOOKSMART: Good evening, Madam.

PATRICIA: Good evening.

LOOKSMART: The dog. It is still here.

PATRICIA: Which dog?

LOOKSMART: The Rottweiler. Chloe – you called it. Still there on the stoep. How is that possible?

PATRICIA: That one is Ethunzini (Zulu for 'shadow').

LOOKSMART: 'Shadow'? Good name. Chloe's puppy, perhaps?

PATRICIA: Chloe died before she could have a pup.

Silence.

LOOKSMART: It doesn't matter. It is still the same dog.

PATRICIA: Do I – know you?

LOOKSMART finally steps into the room. He appears to be in his late thirties. He is dressed in an impeccable suit, with a flagrant red tie.

LOOKSMART: But I am Looksmart. It is just possible you remember me.

28

Silence.

PATRICIA: Looksmart. Why – you've come back! Goodness. And how well you look!

LOOKSMART: As you can see, Madam – I am a different man.

PATRICIA: Yes. You certainly look different. You're wearing a suit.

LOOKSMART enters deeper into room. He laughs quietly.

LOOKSMART: *Yebo*, Madam. This is what I'm like these days. I wear a suit.

He stands there proudly.

But there is an undertone of hostility in him too: whenever he addresses her as Madam, he does so with a bitter irony.

PATRICIA: It took me a moment to recognise you.

LOOKSMART: Because I'm wearing a suit?

PATRICIA: I never thought I'd see you again. How long has it been? I've long ago given up trying to do the Maths – on anything.

LOOKSMART: About fifteen years.

PATRICIA: As long as that?

Silence.

PATRICIA: Times have changed, haven't they?

LOOKSMART: Have they?

PATRICIA: For a start – you're wearing a suit.

LOOKSMART: And you – you are smaller than I remember you. Smaller and – not half as frightening.

PATRICIA: Me? Frightening? I was never that.

LOOKSMART: Ja, ja – I had to look up to you once.

Silence.

He looks about with disbelief.

PATRICIA: Wouldn't you like to sit?

LOOKSMART: Thank you, Madam, but I prefer to stand.

PATRICIA: As you like.

Silence.

PATRICIA: Only the other day I was thinking about you.

LOOKSMART: Oh yes?

PATRICIA: The day you caught your first fish.

Silence.

PATRICIA: Do you remember that?

He turns away, moves off.

PATRICIA: You caught your first fish in the bottom dam.
I bought you a little red fishing rod and taught you to cast
on the front lawn. Don't say you can't remember that?

LOOKSMART: I'm sorry, Madam – but it seems my mind is a
blank.

PATRICIA: We went down to try one afternoon. Just as the
thunder was starting up. I can still see you, running over
the field with the rod held high – like you were tempting
the lightning to strike us. You were so light on your feet.
Like a little bird. Made out of twigs.

LOOKSMART: I was made out of twigs?

PATRICIA: You know what I mean.

LOOKSMART: Not really, Madam.

PATRICIA: The hook kept getting caught everywhere. The
grass, your hair. Even your ear once. But you kept on
going, determined to get a bite. And then at last – you

did! You were so excited, you turned and ran. You ran all the way up the riverbank until the fish came bumping up behind you.

LOOKSMART smiles oddly.

PATRICIA: How I laughed!

BEAUTY enters.

She stares at LOOKSMART.

He barely looks at her.

PATRICIA: We're fine – thank you, Beauty.

BEAUTY leaves.

PATRICIA: You stared down at it. You said how beautiful it looked, flapping there in the dead grass. Then you decided: we had to return it to the water. You remember how we slipped it back? It lay on its back for a while. We thought it was too late. It had taken in too much air. But then it righted itself, flicked its tail and disappeared.

Silence.

PATRICIA: You didn't want to go fishing again after that.

Silence.

LOOKSMART: If I remember myself correctly, I'd have wanted to eat that fish.

PATRICIA: You were a gentle child. Always wanting to please.

LOOKSMART: Don't you mean always wanting to please you?

PATRICIA: Me? Me and everyone else. Even Richard seemed to like you.

LOOKSMART: The Big Baas Richard – liking me? *(With a laugh.)* I certainly don't remember that!

Silence.

PATRICIA: So tell me, Looksmart. How did you come to wear such a smart suit?

LOOKSMART: This isn't fancy dress, Madam. I am not wearing this to please you.

PATRICIA: I know that.

Silence.

He looks again at the wreckage of the room.

PATRICIA: You've caught us here at quite a moment. If you'd come tomorrow, you'd have found us gone.

LOOKSMART: You're leaving tomorrow. Yes – I know all about that.

PATRICIA: You do?

LOOKSMART: Oh yes. I make it my business these days to know about such things. There's a secret network that runs underground. When it pleases me, I put my ear to it.

PATRICIA: That sounds very – mysterious.

LOOKSMART: Oh, it's no mystery.

Silence.

LOOKSMART: So after tomorrow – what are you plans?

PATRICIA: I'm going back to the house where I grew up. By the sea. I'm a Durban girl at heart.

LOOKSMART: *(Another laugh.)* Come, come, Madam. In my head, I can't separate you from this farm.

PATRICIA: Over the years, I might have settled into it. Become accustomed to it. I've become so overgrown with creepers and moss, with old man's beard, that I probably look a part of it. But no – originally I'm not from here.

LOOKSMART looks disappointed.

LOOKSMART: But surely you're going to miss this place?

PATRICIA: Oh, backward glances only crick the neck.

LOOKSMART: So what will you do?

PATRICIA: As little as possible. I plan to spend whole days simply looking at the sea. The ships will be there exactly as I recall them, queuing across the horizon, honking as they come into the harbour. Everything shimmers in Durban. The air, the insects. There are birds in every tree. Have you ever heard the fruit bats?

LOOKSMART: In Durban? I can't say I have.

PATRICIA: They ping.

LOOKSMART: Ping?

PATRICIA: They're as big as turtle doves. My father used to tell me they're the only bats the human ear can actually hear.

LOOKSMART: But what about the Baas? Is he still around? Is he – coming with?

PATRICIA: Of course he is.

LOOKSMART: So what does he say? Won't he miss this place?

PATRICIA: Richard isn't well.

LOOKSMART: *(Pleased.)* Not well, hey? What is it? A heart attack?

PATRICIA: He has a condition. He's losing his mind. I mean – quite literally losing it.

LOOKSMART: And it's too late to find it?

PATRICIA: Far too late to find it.

Silence.

LOOKSMART: It doesn't sound like a very happy ending.

PATRICIA: That's getting old for you.

LOOKSMART: But you've sold the farm. You must be rich.

PATRICIA: Rich? We've been buried in debt for about as long as I can even – think. You know, for every rand the Welsh ponies brought in, Richard's cows and chickens cost another two. And Llewellyn died. You remember Llewellyn?

He shrugs.

PATRICIA: Of course you must. Llewellyn was our very first stallion. All the foals came from him. When he went – my interest in the farm seemed to wane. We sold all the other ponies off to a man in White River. A man who looked very much like yourself. But Richard and I – we can't complain.

LOOKSMART: That's more than can be said for most of us.

She looks at him.

PATRICIA: You don't look as if you've done too badly for yourself.

LOOKSMART: I don't?

PATRICIA: Can't everyone find something to complain about?

LOOKSMART: Like what? Like getting old? Like being rich?

PATRICIA: I see you haven't changed. You're still a child at heart.

He glares at her, furious.

LOOKSMART: Actually I do remember the day we caught that fish. I remember the rock you gave me. To smack its head. You made me hit its head with a rock.

PATRICIA: Nonsense, we let that fish go.

LOOKSMART: You think?

Silence.

LOOKSMART: But I've come around to your way of thinking. I think we do far too much of this – letting people off the hook. Ja, Madam. You'll find I'm a far more effective fisherman now.

He picks up the apple. He picks up the knife.

During the following, he peels the apple into a slow spiral, very carefully.

PATRICIA: You make that sound like a threat.

LOOKSMART: I do? A threat? Well – I'd have to think very carefully about that one. One could argue that it wouldn't be in my interests to threat you.

PATRICIA: One could.

LOOKSMART: One could point out my wife, my two daughters, my car and my well-paying job. Do you know – your former garden boy is now driving a Mercedes-Benz? These days, I'm what you might call a success. Do you want to know how much I paid for this suit?

PATRICIA: I couldn't care less what you paid for that suit.

LOOKSMART: Ja, one could argue that my future is lying ahead of me. Full of promise.

PATRICIA: Looksmart – what is it you want from me?

LOOKSMART: Patience, Madam. Patience is rewarded in the end to those that wait.

Silence.

PATRICIA: You can't come into people's houses and start talking like this.

LOOKSMART: I can't?

PATRICIA: I hardly know who you are anymore.

LOOKSMART: But I thought I hadn't changed.

PATRICIA: In some ways you have –

LOOKSMART: And you? Have you changed?

PATRICIA: Probably. Everything has, hasn't it? The country and everything in it.

35

LOOKSMART: And you're pleased about that?

PATRICIA: My opinion hardly counts.

LOOKSMART: Oh, I'm very interested to know what goes on between your ears.

Silence.

She looks at the knife in his hands.

LOOKSMART: Ja – you're afraid. Like the rest of them, you live in a constant state of fear.

PATRICIA: That's because there are things to be afraid about. Do you know Priscilla Johnson was murdered only last week? Did your network tell you that? They tied her up, raped her and cut her throat. Or maybe they raped her and then tied her up – I wouldn't know.

LOOKSMART: Well I'm glad the truth of this place has finally reached you.

PATRICIA: And you – you're not even a shadow of the little boy I knew. I –

LOOKSMART: Ha! I was hardly a little boy, Madam, I was what? Eighteen when I left?

PATRICIA: You think at eighteen you're a man? Is that what you think?

LOOKSMART: I was a man. You made me to be a man.

PATRICIA: That's something, isn't it?

LOOKSMART: You don't know what I mean!

PATRICIA: How can I! You've being so – perverse!

LOOKSMART: You think I'm a pervert?

PATRICIA: I never said that!

Silence.

LOOKSMART: I have come back here because I have things. *(Indicating head.)* Things in here. Things I can never forget.

PATRICIA: What things? What can they have to do with me?

He looks at the flayed apple and puts it on the mantelpiece.

The knife he still holds in his hand.

LOOKSMART: Do you remember those clay animals I made you once? When I was a boy. No higher than my belt.

PATRICIA: Yes, yes, of course I do.

LOOKSMART: Yes. Yes of course you do. I remember feeling so proud when you put them there, on your mantelpiece. Whenever I came into this room, I'd quickly look up to see if they were still there, in place. After a while they seemed to knock into each other, crack up. I remember a dislodged head, an animal with legs broken off at the knees, lying upside-down on its back. Then one day they were gone.

PATRICIA: You had talent. Are you still doing any art?

LOOKSMART laughs.

LOOKSMART: Madam, I do not have time for such a thing as art. Art? What is the point of that? I was trying to impress you. You call that art?

PATRICIA: You had – something magic in your touch.

LOOKSMART is not convinced.

PATRICIA: It's dark outside. My husband will soon be getting back.

LOOKSMART: I wouldn't count on that.

Silence.

LOOKSMART: But aren't you going to offer me some carrot cake? Isn't that what you usually offer to your guests?

PATRICIA: If you like. Although I'm afraid we don't have any cake. Tea we have. Tea and perhaps some biscuits.

LOOKSMART: That would be nice.

She calls BEAUTY in a more conventional way than she did earlier.

PATRICIA: Beauty!

LOOKSMART: Try it again, Madam.

PATRICIA: Hmm?

LOOKSMART: That isn't how it's usually done.

PATRICIA: I don't know what you're talking about.

LOOKSMART: You know exactly what I'm talking about. She won't come unless you call her like you're calling one of your dogs.

PATRICIA: How dare you!

LOOKSMART: Come on, Madam. Just try it.

PATRICIA: I will not.

LOOKSMART: Try it! Try it again – for old time's sake.

PATRICIA: Beau-ty!

LOOKSMART: Again, Mesis.

PATRICIA: Beau-ty! Beau-ty!

LOOKSMART: That's more like it!

BEAUTY enters.

LOOKSMART: You see? A result!

BEAUTY: Mesis?

PATRICIA: Still no Richard?

BEAUTY: No, Mesis.

PATRICIA: And Bheki?

BEAUTY: I can't find him.

PATRICIA: Keep looking. Bheki must be somewhere.

BEAUTY: I will go, Mesis.

> *LOOKSMART looks at PATRICIA. He mimes drinking a cup of tea.*

PATRICIA: And Beauty – can you prepare some tea. Tea and Marie biscuits, please.

BEAUTY: The biscuits, they have gone soft, Mesis.

PATRICIA: Then put them in the oven. Dry them out.

BEAUTY: I will.

> *BEAUTY is about to leave.*

LOOKSMART: Beauty, *usangikhumbula* (do you remember me)?

BEAUTY: I know you. You are Looksmart.

> *He looks her up and down.*

> *He puts down the knife.*

LOOKSMART: And is that all you have to say? *(To PATRICIA.)* I think she's intimidated by my suit.

> *BEAUTY stares at the ground.*

PATRICIA: Thank you, Beauty. Just the tea.

BEAUTY: *Yebo*, Mesis.

> *BEAUTY glances at the knife and leaves.*

LOOKSMART: She was a small girl when I saw her last. Now she looks like an old woman. How is that possible?

PATRICIA: She keeps herself to herself. She and Bheki will be coming with us to Durban tomorrow.

> *Silence.*

PATRICIA: Looksmart – please tell me what you want.

LOOKSMART: I knew her older sister better. Her name was Grace.

Silence.

LOOKSMART: A lot like Beauty, only far more beautiful.

PATRICIA: The girl who died. You –

LOOKSMART: Died or was killed? Which was it? *(Off her look.)* You do not like the distinction? At the time, I saw it as murder. Plain and simple.

PATRICIA: Murder?

LOOKSMART: Mur-der.

Silence.

PATRICIA: Looksmart –

LOOKSMART: That is not my name.

PATRICIA: What?

LOOKSMART: Looksmart is not my name.

Silence.

PATRICIA: But I was there when you were born. I was there at the exact moment your mother named you Looksmart.

LOOKSMART: Ag – stop your lies. You're a bloody liar, Madam!

PATRICIA: *(Trying to claw her way back at him.)* It was a wet night – like this. Richard had gone off on one of his errands and your father – he banged on the door. I thought it was the wind at first, but then I went there and I found your father. He said I must come. He said his child – you – were ready to be born. So I followed him out. The rain stinging our faces. But I found my way in the darkness, all the way to your parents' hut.

LOOKSMART: You're making this up!

PATRICIA: I am pain – that's what your mother said. She looked all twisted up, like a wet towel. I told her the pain was her friend. It was there to get the baby out.

Don't scream, I said. Instead you must push. And it took another hour – of screaming and not screaming – until out you came, grey and rubbery, like a big dead fish. But you weren't dead. I lifted you up and you screamed and everyone laughed. We knew then that you would be alright.

LOOKSMART shakes his head, but he is hanging onto every word she says.

PATRICIA: I wrapped you in a bundle and handed you to your mother and you found her breast and started to suck. Even though the milk hadn't come, you knew what you wanted and where to find it. A strong chap you'll be, I said. And your mother said, We will name him Looksmart. Usually – I would have left. But I sat by the bed and me and your parents had some tea. We stared at your tiny sleeping face for so long that all other faces looked impossibly huge, like exaggerated moons. It was a good night to be born, Looksmart. The rain went deep. It felt like nothing wicked would ever be left in the world.

Silence.

LOOKSMART starts to pace the room.

LOOKSMART: My name is Phiwayinkosi Ndlovu. That is the name my parents gave me! But only when you were gone again. Looksmart – that is only the name they gave in order to please you! But I am not here for this. I am here to talk about Grace. Grace. The sister of Beauty. The girl I loved!

PATRICIA: The girl you loved? But – I don't know anything about that.

LOOKSMART: Well – you wouldn't!

PATRICIA: Listen to me – people get attacked by dogs all the time. It's a terrible thing, but it's not – it's not murder.

BEAUTY enters with the tea and biscuits.

LOOKSMART: God – you should be stuffed and put in a museum!

BEAUTY sets the tray down on the table next to PATRICIA. She switches on the lamp.

BEAUTY: *Nanti itiye* (here is the tea), Mesis.

She pours the tea for PATRICIA and gives her the cup and saucer.

PATRICIA: *Ngiyabonga*, Beauty.

BEAUTY: I will go again and look for uBaas.

BEAUTY starts to leave.

LOOKSMART: I'll have mine with milk.

BEAUTY stops. Then she turns back and pours LOOKSMART's tea. She leaves it on a box near him.

LOOKSMART: And sugar. Three and a bit.

BEAUTY returns to the tray, gets the sugar, dumps three spoons into his cup. She leaves the teaspoon there but doesn't stir it.

Then she picks up the knife and slips it into her pocket.

PATRICIA: Thank you, Beauty.

BEAUTY leaves.

LOOKSMART picks up his tea, stirs it, sips.

LOOKSMART: The big Baas Richard! When I think of him, I think of a soft, white moth. Small, weak, without any blood. When I take him between my finger and my thumb to find out what is there, I find he has just turned to dust.

Silence.

PATRICIA: Looksmart, I hope you haven't made some terrible mistake.

LOOKSMART: *(Putting down the tea.)* What I want is for you to tell me. To tell me everything you remember about this girl – Grace!

PATRICIA: But I hardly said two words –

LOOKSMART: Because I can see it all quite clearly. We are sitting – you and me – just out there on the stoep. When we hear this animal cry, coming from there – from the dairy. And then nothing. You turn to me and ask me what is happening when we see her – running along the dirt track past the house. *(Gesturing beyond the room.)* Right – there. Her clothing in tatters. Did you ever wonder why her clothing was in tatters?

PATRICIA: She was – half-dressed.

LOOKSMART: And you never wondered about that?

PATRICIA: It was the police's job. To wonder about that.

LOOKSMART: I was actually waiting for her to come to your house that morning. She wanted to ask for time off. For the wedding. For preparations. But she never did ask, did she?

PATRICIA: The – wedding?

LOOKSMART: At first I can't believe what I'm seeing. Her head down, not wasting any breath for screaming. And then the dog, the Baas's dog, black and silent, galloping fast. Three, then two, then one pace behind her.

PATRICIA: Richard said it had broken free.

LOOKSMART: Suddenly, Grace is a double creature. Half woman, half dog. She utters a sound so terrible I don't even recognise it as her, as coming from her. But it brings a dozen farmworkers into the garden within seconds. We gather around, worshippers around some – ancient sacrifice. Silent with terror. Whenever I try to approach, the dog swivels around so that Grace stands between us. Always, always, Grace is coming between us. And Grace, she is wailing in a strange, song-like way. She utters the same few notes repeatedly, obsessively, as if her voice has found the right level, the right pitch, the right song for the pain.

PATRICIA: I didn't hear that. I was getting the gun. I tried to get a clear shot. Didn't you hear the shot I fired into the air?

LOOKSMART: There was nothing like that.

PATRICIA: I went in and pulled the dog away when it was adjusting its grip!

LOOKSMART: She stares ahead –

PATRICIA: Afterwards, I wanted to shoot that dog. But my husband stopped me. He said she'd been taunting it, throwing stones at it, and that it pulled itself free.

LOOKSMART: I wrap her up in an old horse blanket and carry her towards your car. But you don't want me to put her there. You think her blood will ruin the seats. You don't say it, but I can see you – thinking it. You tell us to carry her across to the dairy. To take her to the hospital in the back of the bakkie. But when we get there, there is no bakkie. So I come back and tell you. You agree to let me put her in your car. The Mercedes-Benz. You make us put down lots of blankets on the back seat. We lay her down. I drive, fast as I can, to the nearest hospital. When we get there, I think she's fallen into a deep sleep. But she's not asleep, is she? She is dead.

Silence.

LOOKSMART: I only stayed on the farm long enough to see them bury her. When I left the next morning, the clouds were – torn to pieces across the sky.

PATRICIA: That poor girl. If she hadn't thrown that stone –

LOOKSMART: That stone? Ha! Who threw the first stone, Madam?

PATRICIA stares at him.

LOOKSMART: What I've told you is not the full story. It is only what we saw. What about what we didn't see?

Silence.

LOOKSMART: When I was carrying Grace towards the dairy, her mouth against my ear, she whispered something so bad that I have never told it to anyone. It was your husband.

Your husband Richard who caused it. Beauty saw them. She walked into that room where the milk tank is. She found them there. On the floor.

PATRICIA: I beg your pardon?

LOOKSMART: Your husband was holding her down and raping her.

PATRICIA: Don't be –

LOOKSMART: He never saw Beauty, but Grace did. She uttered that shriek we heard and she shoved him off.

PATRICIA: I don't believe one word of –

LOOKSMART: Ja, but Beauty must have seen another thing. She saw your husband unchain the dog and let it loose in Grace.

PATRICIA: What?

LOOKSMART: He unchained the dog and climbed into his bakkie and he drove away into the hills.

Silence.

PATRICIA: You are calling Richard a murderer.

LOOKSMART: I believe that's exactly what I am calling him.

PATRICIA: It is not a word to use lightly.

LOOKSMART: Do you think I am using it lightly?

Silence.

PATRICIA: I simply can't – Beauty said nothing. She never has.

LOOKSMART: After Grace's death, I just left. Who would the police have believed: your husband or me? If I'd stayed, I might have killed him. I might have buried my hands deep inside of him and drawn out his heart. His heart for my heart.

PATRICIA: Richard was far too much of a –

LOOKSMART: Too much of a racist to fuck a black girl? Evidently not.

45

PATRICIA: Even if it's true. Even if he did have sex with her – God knows, he might have, he tried to sleep with a long line of stable girls out from England – even then you simply don't know he set the dog on her. That's a monstrous thing to say. Especially when you don't know the facts.

LOOKSMART: What facts?

PATRICIA: The girl was – she was throwing the stones. And the dog broke free and attacked her. Yes. And after, when I'd dragged the dog into the house – there was nothing at all about going to the dairy to get the bakkie. We loaded her straight into the Merc and drove her away at once!

LOOKSMART: I carried her, didn't I? You hid in the house.

PATRICIA: I went to call the hospital, get more blankets – who knows what?

LOOKSMART: Exact –

PATRICIA: And how can you possibly know what I was thinking? I doubt very much that I was thinking! But I know this: I would never cared about getting blood in the seats!

LOOKSMART: You're going to deny even that?

PATRICIA: By your own admission I never even said it!

LOOKSMART: You thought it! You said we had to take her to the bakkie. And when she had to go in your car, you made us to put down blankets – flea-bitten blankets you reserve for your dogs! Of course you thought it, maan!

Silence.

PATRICIA: Listen, Looksmart. I don't know what happened. Or why it has to matter now. Can't you see – you're wasting your time on this. On me. On things that are dead. You have a wife now. Children. You have a splendid bloody suit!

LOOKSMART: But I want you to understand!

PATRICIA: What?

LOOKSMART: What I understand.

Silence.

LOOKSMART: The first thing I saw on getting back from boarding school was a black puppy. Playing in the garden. Chewing a rubber ball to bits. The second was Grace. The most beautiful thing I have ever seen. As our love grew, that dog in the garden was growing too. My love and your fear. They grew together. And now I can no longer separate them. When I think of one, I see the other. I see that double thing. The beast. Circling the garden, dripping blood.

PATRICIA: But – what can I say to that? Do you expect me to change it? Make it all – better?

LOOKSMART: You gave up. You withdrew at the exact moment it was your chance to step forward. Do something. Save her.

PATRICIA: I did save her. I tried. I pulled the dog away. I got it back into the house.

LOOKSMART: I thought you cared, but you didn't. I thought I meant something, but I didn't. All you cared about was protecting your seats!

PATRICIA: I don't know what you're trying to say, Looksmart. Can't you see that all of this – it's lost.

LOOKSMART: Lost? It isn't lost. I think about it every day.

Silence.

He is almost weeping.

PATRICIA: The shame. The shame of it. Oh, I don't know. That dog was trying to please us, that's all. It had learned that. To be like that. From the country. Richard. Me. A poison we have, we grow up with. Now it's been passed on to you. The dream of the dog. The dream of the dog doing its work. Destroying everything.

LOOKSMART: But you must pay. You must pay for what you've done.

Silence.

PATRICIA: Believe me, I do.

BEAUTY enters. She is dripping wet, her feet covered in mud.

BEAUTY: Mesis, I have looked everywhere and I can't find uBaas.

PATRICIA: Beauty, I want to ask you.

BEAUTY: Mesis?

PATRICIA: I want to ask about your sister. Grace.

BEAUTY: *Yebo*, Mesis?

PATRICIA: I want you to tell me what happened the day she died. And I want the truth.

BEAUTY: *Yebo*, Mesis.

PATRICIA: You have nothing to be afraid of.

BEAUTY: *Yebo*, Mesis.

Silence.

BEAUTY: The dog outside. It killed her.

PATRICIA: Yes, but before that. At the dairy. What did you see?

BEAUTY: *Lutho* (Nothing), Mesis.

PATRICIA: Then why do you look so afraid?

LOOKSMART: *Ungesabi* (Don't be afraid), Beauty. *Siyalazi iqiniso* (We know the truth).

BEAUTY: *(To LOOKSMART.)* You do not know the truth.

PATRICIA: You must not be afraid.

BEAUTY: Mesis, I can't say.

PATRICIA: You know Richard. He is a sick man now. You are the only one who saw the whole of what happened and still remembers.

BEAUTY: I was a small girl then, Mesis. I am not sure of what I saw.

PATRICIA: I won't blame you. For telling me. I promise you that. Beauty – please. You must speak!

BEAUTY: I was finishing with the cows, letting them out into the – I was about to do the cleaning with the hosepipe and – and – and –

PATRICIA: And?

BEAUTY: I was turning on the tap when – the noise, it is coming from the storage room. So I open the door a little bit, very soft, so I can see – and then I see.

PATRICIA: What do you see, Beauty?

LOOKSMART: They're on the floor, aren't they?

BEAUTY: Yes.

LOOKSMART: His hand over her mouth.

BEAUTY: She sees me and –

LOOKSMART: *Qhubeka* (Carry on), Beauty!

PATRICIA: Did she get away from him then?

BEAUTY: *Yebo*, Mesis.

PATRICIA: The dog. Did Richard unchain the dog?

BEAUTY: He undo the chain and the dog running –

LOOKSMART: Ja. He waits to see the dog catch her, doesn't he? He waits to make sure. Isn't that it, Beauty?

BEAUTY: That – is it.

LOOKSMART moves away, satisfied.

PATRICIA: Why didn't you tell the police?

BEAUTY: I was afraid.

PATRICIA: Does Richard know what you saw?

BEAUTY: No one knows what I saw.

PATRICIA: Did ever try anything – with you?

BEAUTY: *Cha* (No), Mesis. uGrace was the last one. From the farm.

Silence.

PATRICIA: Thank you, Beauty. We won't speak about this again.

BEAUTY: *Ngiyabonga*, Mesis.

Silence.

BEAUTY: But what about uBaas? Do you still want him?

The ambiguity hangs in the air.

PATRICIA: *(To LOOKSMART.)* What have you done to him?

LOOKSMART: I have not seen your husband yet. It was to you I came to speak.

PATRICIA turns back to BEAUTY.

PATRICIA: Thank you, Beauty.

BEAUTY nods and leaves.

Silence.

PATRICIA: Looksmart – I think I owe you an apology.

LOOKSMART: You think?

PATRICIA: But – neither can I undo what has happened. What Richard has done, he has done. And I will never be able to take back that terrible thought I had – you say I had – when that young girl lay bleeding.

LOOKSMART: Yet, you are sorry?

PATRICIA: Yes, I am sorry. Even if that doesn't seem enough.

LOOKSMART: Enough? Enough for what?

PATRICIA: For you to walk away from here. For you to go out and try to become – something new. I suppose I'm only asking about hope.

LOOKSMART: Hope? Ag, I've tested that one out. And what do you see? The picture of success. A man in a suit. A car, wife, two children. Everything I've ever done, I've done it with hope.

PATRICIA: That's not so bad, is it? I never managed to have a child.

LOOKSMART: There's more to a man than a suit!

PATRICIA: What – are you saying you aren't gratified by your success?

LOOKSMART: I am saying that I wish for you guilt! Darkness! I don't want you to leave this place without a backwards glance. To spend your last days looking at – at the sea – with your mind all clear, your sleep easy! I want you to remember that dog like I remember that dog, and I want you to be haunted and – and – and – decayed away by it!

Silence.

PATRICIA: I do understand how you feel.

LOOKSMART: Rubbish!

PATRICIA: I know what it is. To die quietly.

LOOKSMART: Rubbish.

Silence.

PATRICIA: I married him because I was pregnant. My father wanted to kill him when he heard, but I talked to him and he gave us this farm instead. He was a good man, my father. Perhaps the only good man in my life. And when he died, he died thinking I was happy, hoping I was happy, taking my word for it. You were a small boy then. Always hanging around the house. And I think I was happy then. Happy for a bit.

LOOKSMART: You told me you never managed to have a child.

PATRICIA: What?

LOOKSMART: But he made you pregnant.

PATRICIA: I did have one.

LOOKSMART: And this one child – it is still alive or what?

PATRICIA: I think that is my business.

LOOKSMART: *(Losing it again.)* Well – I want to make it my business! I want to know about this child. Because once – a long time ago – I thought you cared about another child. You sent me to that fancy school, you gave me that blazer, corrected all my English. You woke something up and then killed it. You killed it as surely as you made me to kill that fish!

PATRICIA: We let that fish go!

LOOKSMART: We didn't.

PATRICIA: We did!

LOOKSMART: We didn't!

Silence.

PATRICIA: I gave you everything you ever asked for.
You wanted to go to that boarding school, so I sent you. Don't you remember the trunk full of tuck? The labels me and your mother sewed on? The letters. Remember the letters you used to write? Every Sunday evening, for five years, I wrote back.

LOOKSMART: And every holiday I came home to sleep in my mud hut.

PATRICIA: Well how would your mother have felt – her sleeping over there and you here with us?

LOOKSMART: And I'm sure your husband would have welcomed me in!

PATRICIA: Well I did what I could. And you were there every morning. Standing on the stoep. Always wanting to help. So I taught you all about my roses. I would give you work to get on with – pruning, mulching, dead-heading. And when you were done you would clean my car – every square inch of it.

LOOKSMART: And give me some small change for my efforts.

PATRICIA: It's quite natural to earn some pocket money, you know. *(Off his look.)* And in the end when I taught you to drive that car, you loved it! Don't tell me you didn't love it! And don't tell me you didn't love your school! What would you have preferred? Staying here – herding cows, mucking out? Because that's what would have happened. Swallowing your anger, illiterate, working for him! Sending you to that school was the one good thing I did with my life. I tried to do one good thing. One good act against a great tide of – filth!

LOOKSMART: Tell me about your son!

PATRICIA: What?

LOOKSMART: What happened to your son?

PATRICIA: Who said anything about a son?

LOOKSMART: What?

PATRICIA: It was a girl who died, not a son.

LOOKSMART: And?

PATRICIA: She was born.

LOOKSMART: And?

PATRICIA: There were complications.

Silence.

PATRICIA: She was born dead.

Long silence.

PATRICIA: They brought her for me to look at. All clean and wrapped, like a gift. But there was no mistaking she was dead. Her little blue eyelids, shut firmly against the world. She was perfect. The only thing she lacked was a life.

LOOKSMART turns away from her.

PATRICIA: She was made of wax. She glowed. As if there was a cold yellow moon inside of her – instead of a heart. She was so defenceless, lying there. The way her little head flopped back. Abandoned to the world. Rachel would be forever dead.

Silence.

PATRICIA: The nurse brought her back later in a box the size for shoes. I carried her out into another day. A long path ahead of me. With her death at the beginning of it and my death at the end of it. Nothing else in between.

LOOKSMART: You buried her on the hill.

PATRICIA: Looking out towards Giant's Castle.

LOOKSMART: Ja.

PATRICIA: I'd made a bedroom for her. All painted white. A wooden changing table, drawers filled with baby clothes and blankets. I'd had my old pram brought up from Durban for wheeling her around the house. When I was a baby, I'd come up here with my parents. I would have my afternoon nap under the fir trees at the front, with the weavers chattering high above me. I wanted the same for her.

LOOKSMART: What about Richard?

PATRICIA: There's nothing much to say about Richard.
After the burial, he barely looked at me. I don't think
he's ever really looked at me since.

LOOKSMART: And you?

PATRICIA: I sat here in this chair. For about a thousand years.

LOOKSMART: You didn't try again – for another child?

PATRICIA: It would have had to come through divine
intervention.

They almost smile.

PATRICIA: Anyway, there was a farm to run. I had to start
trying to make some money as Richard seemed so intent
on losing it. So I bred Welsh ponies. For other people's
children. I became the most successful breeder in the
country for a while. And then one morning – there you
were. Running down the corridor like you already owned
the place.

LOOKSMART says nothing.

PATRICIA: Didn't you know? You were the only child to be
happy in this house.

LOOKSMART: I didn't.

PATRICIA: You were like the sun. My son. I never asked you to
come into my life – but you did. As if we'd been connected
since that night you were born. As if some part of you
remembered. When your teacher suggested we send you
to a better school, I didn't hesitate. We walked around the
grounds with the headmaster. You lit up. Said you wanted
to go there more than anything. So you went. You'd come
back here at the weekends full of stories. And full of
mischief, I might add. I started to call you Mr Monologue.

He smiles.

PATRICIA: Until one day you started to look at everything
with different eyes. The photographs, the horses, even the

55

car. You'd started to judge us. Oh the weight of it – after such lightness! I thought it was adolescence. I hoped it would pass. But it didn't. Then Grace. Then you vanished. Did I connect your disappearance and Grace? I might have. I tried to ask your mother about it – your sudden departure – but I got nothing out of her. A few years later she vanished too.

Silence.

PATRICIA: You know what I would have said if you'd told me you wanted to marry Grace?

He waits for her to continue.

PATRICIA: I would have told you that you could do better. You must never marry below yourself. That's what I did with Richard.

LOOKSMART: And now? What would you say if I wanted to marry her now?

PATRICIA: Who knows? I never knew her.

Silence.

PATRICIA: Where's your mother now?

LOOKSMART: With me. In a cottage at the bottom of our garden. Up there in Johannesburg. You know she grows mealies and spinach in our garden? She says she doesn't like all that wasted space.

PATRICIA smiles.

PATRICIA: And did she know about Grace – you and Grace?

LOOKSMART: Something of it, perhaps.

PATRICIA: I could never understand it. The way you went off. I had to think of you as another dead child.

Silence.

LOOKSMART: I had to hold tight to my anger that day. In order to leave like that. I know it must have hurt.

PATRICIA: I survived. You manage to walk things off after a bit.

Silence.

LOOKSMART: I could have been a good man. Like your father.

PATRICIA: You have to get rid of – all this.

LOOKSMART: There are people out there who think I am a good man. My wife. My daughters. You see, I am liked. I have always been liked. Since you first liked me, I have been liked.

She smiles.

PATRICIA: What is your wife like?

LOOKSMART: Like you say your father was.

PATRICIA: You have been happy?

LOOKSMART: Sometimes.

Silence.

LOOKSMART: Do you know what will happen to this farm after you're gone?

PATRICIA: It's going to some big land development company.

LOOKSMART: *Yebo.* The company I work for.

PATRICIA: You work for them?

LOOKSMART: *Yebo.*

PATRICIA: How extraordinary!

LOOKSMART: *Yebo*, Madam. I have come back here – yes. But not to take back the land that was taken from my people – no. But to establish a gated community. It's for the whites and Indians who are fleeing the cities. They say they're trying to get away from the crime, but I think it's us they don't like – the blacks. Have you seen the plans?

PATRICIA: No.

LOOKSMART makes a table out of a box and an old framed picture and spreads out a map, which he has taken from an inside pocket.

LOOKSMART: Come. Come see for yourself.

She moves towards the map.

PATRICIA: What will happen to the house? I hope they knock it down, brick by brick.

LOOKSMART: The house will be left on top of the hill. We will cut down the gum trees around it to open things up a little. The place needs light. A view of the Drakensberg – *izintaba zoKhahlamba* (the Zulu name for the Drakensberg)!

PATRICIA: The trees were there to protect us from the wind.

LOOKSMART: Stylistically, the house has a vernacular value all of its own. We plan to reproduce it a dozen times, with slight variations, all across the valley.

LOOKSMART moves away from the map.

LOOKSMART: The hills I knew so well will be buried in pine plantations. The wetlands will be turned into dams for farming trout. All those birds that surrounded me as a boy – that rainbow that always twittered – it will slowly fade. One morning there will be only silence.

PATRICIA: How terrible.

LOOKSMART: The hut I was born in, that will go too. Along with all the other farm buildings. Do you know how long it takes a machine to flatten a mud hut? It's the work of weeks to build it. But it can be gone again before you can even cry for help. Ja – everything will go except this house. This house will remain alone. But it will be transformed beyond recognition. There will be pale wooden floors, sliding doors, skylights. The stoep extended all around. A turret structure will be added to the north wall for what we call a vertical focus. Ah Madam – you will see. We will whisk this place into something you'd never imagine. Not even in your wildest – nightmares.

PATRICIA: I think it sounds rather lovely. We should have done all that years ago.

LOOKSMART: Open plan. Yes.

PATRICIA: But how did you become involved in all this?

LOOKSMART: When the sale of this farm reached my ears, I made sure I'd be involved in developing it. I wanted to cut it all up. All the things I've never spoken about. Not even to my wife. Do you know – I have never mentioned your name to any single soul?

PATRICIA: Well tomorrow we'll be gone. You can finally clear yourself of everything that's dead.

LOOKSMART: Dead? Now that I'm here, I feel different about it. At one point, you know – I think I loved you.

PATRICIA: You did?

LOOKSMART: I loved you more than my own mother.

Long silence.

LOOKSMART: Whenever I talked about the school she would look at me with strange eyes. With the same eyes she used when she looked at you.

PATRICIA: But you know she often talked about you. We'd sit at the table in the kitchen, the back door open, the puppy snapping up flies – and the letter telling us you'd been made a prefect always in her apron pocket. I'd have to read that letter over and over for her. She was so proud she couldn't speak. We both were.

LOOKSMART: By the end of it I fitted nowhere. Not with you, not with her.

PATRICIA: Perhaps that's the price you had to pay. You and your mother.

LOOKSMART: Perhaps it's the price you had to pay too.

PATRICIA: Perhaps.

Silence.

LOOKSMART refolds the plans, returns them to his pocket.

PATRICIA: One day you think you might come and visit?

LOOKSMART: At your house by the sea?

PATRICIA: Why not?

LOOKSMART: We could find ourselves an old Rottweiler. Take it for walks along the beech.

PATRICIA: We could throw sticks for it.

LOOKSMART: Make it jump through hoops.

They smile.

PATRICIA: Anyway – I'm glad you came. It's been good to get to know you a little.

LOOKSMART: You know nothing about me. A few words – that's all.

PATRICIA: Sometimes a few words can be enough. To know what a person is.

LOOKSMART: Ah Madam – this is a strange land we live in. For your generation, you white people, you still want to be the mothers and fathers, and we – we must be something like your children. But that relationship can have no place in the future of this country.

PATRICIA: Yet you were like my son, Looksmart. At least as close as I ever got to having one. *(Off his look.)* And I'll be lonely there, in my house by the sea. I really would like you to visit. Even if it is just to humour an old *gogo* (grandmother) with one or two marbles still rolling around inside her head.

LOOKSMART: If I come, I can come with clay animals I've made so you can look at them and think – it's art!

PATRICIA: And I will bake a carrot cake. What I usually offer to my guests.

Outside, RICHARD is approaching.

RICHARD: She hasn't fed the bloody dog!

PATRICIA: Then feed it yourself!

He goes off again – without entering the room.

PATRICIA: Looksmart, there's something I want you to promise me. Something I want you to protect.

LOOKSMART: I think I understand. The grave on the hill?

PATRICIA: Rachel. Yes.

LOOKSMART: I used to go there and sit under the beefwoods, looking across to Giant's Castle. That's a good resting place.

PATRICIA: I don't want to disturb it.

LOOKSMART: When I used to see that grey rock with the name on it, I thought it was from another time – from before you and Richard. I never thought to ask you about it.

PATRICIA: I didn't want that shadow – to come between us.

LOOKSMART: Well the grave will be safe, Madam. I will make sure it remains protected.

PATRICIA: Thank you. My worst nightmare is the bulldozers. Digging her up.

She touches his hand lightly, sealing a pact.

RICHARD: *(Shouting off again.)* And where the hell is Bheki?

PATRICIA: He's been trying to look for her. He wants to dig her up.

RICHARD: I think he's buggered off!

They smile.

LOOKSMART: Do you remember that time I over-watered your roses? I made them go yellow. All the leaves fell off. You tried your best to be nice about it, but hell – you were cross!

They laugh.

RICHARD has entered. He is drenched and covered in mud. In his arms, he's carrying a beautiful basalt rock. It looks like an enormous speckled bird's egg.

RICHARD: What is going on?

PATRICIA: *(Referring to the rock.)* What is that, Richard?

RICHARD: I rooted around, but there was nothing there.

PATRICIA: Oh God – what have you done?

RICHARD: I thought the house was burning as I was digging in the dark.

LOOKSMART doesn't move towards him. He watches, his face blank.

RICHARD: Beauty came and called for me. I thought something terrible had happened. Her voice wailing in the wind. I understood at last that we'd all be dead. But we aren't dead, are we?

PATRICIA says nothing.

RICHARD: *(Finally turning to LOOKSMART.)* Who the hell is this?

PATRICIA: The surveyor. He works for the land development company. He was about to leave.

RICHARD: Isn't it a bit late for this?

LOOKSMART steps forward. He takes the muddy rock from RICHARD and places it on the mantelpiece.

LOOKSMART: It's never too late for this.

He wipes his hands on an old rag nearby. Throughout the following, he is almost buoyant – as if RICHARD no longer has any power over him.

RICHARD: *(To PATRICIA.)* What does he want?

LOOKSMART: So you don't recognise me?

RICHARD: Should I?

LOOKSMART: I am Phiwayinkosi Ndlovu, *Gatsheni, boya benyathi busongwa, busombuluka zidlekhaya ngoba ziswele abelusi – Ngonyama* (Ndlovu clan names)! But I think you knew me once as Looksmart.

RICHARD: Looksmart? And where is it we met?

LOOKSMART: Right here. On this farm. Some years ago.

RICHARD: I've never heard of any Looksmart. What kind of a name is that?

LOOKSMART: It is a name like Baas is a name.

RICHARD: What are you doing wearing a suit? Did someone die?

LOOKSMART: I came to shed a bit of light.

RICHARD: You remind me of my Uncle Pete. Have you ever met my Uncle Pete?

LOOKSMART: I haven't had that pleasure – no.

RICHARD: Well, let me tell you a little story about my Uncle Pete. The last time I saw him, he was dying, here, on this carpet, wearing a suit! Poor bugger had a food allergy. Peanuts! So he says to me, he says, 'Richard, I have something terrible to confess.' 'Don't worry, Pete,' I say, 'You tell me and get it all off your chest.' So he says, 'Over the past years, whenever I've come to stay, I've been going into your daughter's room at night and I've been holding her down and I've been fucking her!'

PATRICIA: Jesus!

LOOKSMART: Your what?

RICHARD: *(To PATRICIA.)* Your daughter!

PATRICIA: How dare you!

RICHARD: *(To PATRICIA.)* Are you going to listen to this story, or what? Anyway, so I tell him, 'Listen, Pete, it's all in the past now. Let's forgive and forget. We'll put it all behind us and carry on. But Pete,' I tell him, 'now that we're deciding to confess and all, I've got something to say to you. I'm the one who put the peanuts in the sherry trifle!'

RICHARD laughs at his joke.

LOOKSMART looks back steadily.

LOOKSMART: I think I shall leave you to your wife.

He turns his back on RICHARD.

RICHARD: You know, there was a time when I would have had you whipped!

LOOKSMART: Good night to you, Pa-tri-shi-a.

PATRICIA: A new start?

LOOKSMART: I'm a heavy bull, with three bellies to feed. The rest of my life belongs to my family. And the manager of the bank.

RICHARD: A real man isn't scared of a bit of debt!

PATRICIA: One day – the beach? We'll throw sticks?

LOOKSMART: Me and dogs –

PATRICIA: Carrot cake?

RICHARD: What on earth are you two on about?

LOOKSMART: *Sala kahle* (Stay well), Mama. Don't worry – I'll let myself out.

LOOKSMART leaves.

PATRICIA: *(To herself.) Hamba kahle* (Go well), Phiwayinkosi.

RICHARD: Who did he say he was? He said he knew me. He said we'd met before, I think.

PATRICIA: It doesn't matter now.

PATRICIA looks at the stone on the mantelpiece.

PATRICIA: What did you do to her?

RICHARD: What?

PATRICIA: Rooted around, did you? Like a pig in the dark! Why couldn't you leave her alone?

RICHARD: There was nothing there. Just a thin twig, some rotten fruit. So I covered it up.

PATRICIA: It? She's not an it! Say her name, Richard!

RICHARD: What?

PATRICIA: Say her name! Rachel!

RICHARD: No.

PATRICIA: Say Grace.

RICHARD: What?

PATRICIA: Grace! Grace! Say the name Grace!

RICHARD: What are you trying to say?

PATRICIA: Grace!

RICHARD: Why? What do you want to do to me? Didn't they say I was to avoid all stress? You're trying to kill me. Is that what you want?

PATRICIA: I could see very clearly that you recognised him, Richard. You aren't half as bloody senile as you pretend to be.

RICHARD: Well of course I remember Looksmart! I said at the time it was a mistake. But you didn't listen to me. You never did. You only ever listened to your father.

PATRICIA: That's because he was worth listening to.

RICHARD: And what have you created in the end? Looksmart! He looks like a bloody twat to me, in his fucking suit!

PATRICIA: That fucking suit now owns this place!

RICHARD: What's he going to do? Open a shebeen?

PATRICIA: You tell me, Richard. You tell me what you did to Grace.

RICHARD: It was a lie. Designed to upset me. I never believed a word of it. I never believed we could have made – that.

PATRICIA: What on earth are you talking about?

RICHARD: There's nothing more to say. It was all a trick. A twist. A knife in my back. How many times do I have to say it?

PATRICIA: Don't you want to give yourself some peace?

RICHARD: There's never any peace.

PATRICIA is staring at him steadily – an insect on a pin.

RICHARD: There was no name for it, alright?

PATRICIA: Say it, Richard. No name for what?

RICHARD: You don't actually know, do you?

PATRICIA: I know what I need to know. You unleashed the dog. You murdered her.

RICHARD: Oh. But is that all?

PATRICIA: Good God! Isn't that enough?

RICHARD: She was a lying bitch.

PATRICIA: Don't you feel any remorse?

RICHARD: To you? I did nothing to you, did I?

PATRICIA: To her, Richard! To Grace!

RICHARD: Are you mad?

PATRICIA: Oh, I can't bear to look at you!

RICHARD: Who are you anyway? What makes you the judge? All perched up – looking down at me! You putrid –

PATRICIA: Go. Leave. Get out! Out! Just get out of my sight!

RICHARD leaves.

BEAUTY finally enters.

BEAUTY: Mesis?

PATRICIA: He's gone.

BEAUTY: *Yebo*, Mesis.

PATRICIA: I never thanked him properly.

BEAUTY: Mesis?

PATRICIA: For – helping me.

BEAUTY: *(Drawing PATRICIA towards the chair.) Kulungile* (It's okay), Mesis. He will understand.

PATRICIA sits.

PATRICIA: Are we ready to go?

BEAUTY: *Cha*, Mesis. I don't think so. *Sisaqedelela* (We haven't finished).

PATRICIA: All these years. And you never said a word. Come, Beauty. Talk to me.

PATRICIA pushes across a box for BEAUTY to sit on. BEAUTY sits uneasily.

PATRICIA: Why? Why did you stay here? Why did you remain silent?

BEAUTY: This is where I live. This job is good for me. My family has always lived here.

PATRICIA: Aren't you angry about what happened to Grace?

BEAUTY: I was a child. I didn't know if I should be angry. We do not talk about uSisGrace. We think of her as something – lost.

PATRICIA: Beauty, tell me the truth.

BEAUTY: Why?

PATRICIA: I have to know.

BEAUTY: Another day will be better.

PATRICIA: No. Now. Today.

BEAUTY: uSisGrace. She was with uBaas.

PATRICIA: Yes?

BEAUTY: She was together with him some other times before.

PATRICIA waits for her to continue.

BEAUTY: uBaas, he would pay her money each and every time. They said that Grace, she never loved Looksmart. Not like Looksmart loved her. He was too young for her. His head had too much words inside it. She said to my mother she was not wanting to marry him.

PATRICIA: But he said they loved each other. He said she was good.

BEAUTY: She had nothing, and uBaas, he paid her. Grace did not think about good or not good. *Ubezama ukuphila* (She was trying to survive).

PATRICIA: She was trying to survive?

BEAUTY: *Yebo.*

PATRICIA: Go on, Beauty.

BEAUTY: When she died, Grace was pregnant with uBaas's child.

PATRICIA: She was – ?

DREAM OF THE DOG

BEAUTY: *Yebo*, Mesis.

Silence.

PATRICIA: What about Richard? Did he know?

BEAUTY: Before she died, Grace told him. It was at the dairy, in that room they went to. He was angry. Because she wanted to keep it. The child. She told him it was against her customs, her religion, to kill a child. I heard it from outside the door, listening. Then he started to swear. He hit her. I could see it through the door. She pushed him and she ran away, screaming about the child. And uBaas, he freed his dog on her.

PATRICIA: My God. You saw this?

BEAUTY: *Yebo*, Mesis.

Silence.

PATRICIA: Why didn't you tell Looksmart about it now?

BEAUTY: Looksmart would not be able to hear something like that.

PATRICIA: I see that, yes. But Looksmart has his own story. He's very persuasive about it. Must I now believe you?

BEAUTY: Mesis, you must find the truth for yourself.

Silence.

PATRICIA: He killed Grace. He said there was no name for it. He said, 'Is that all?' It wasn't, was it? She was pregnant. He murdered two people. Grace and his child. The ambulance is coming. There are two dead children for you to pick up. My God – he killed his own flesh and blood.

BEAUTY: I don't think uBaas can see it like that, Mesis. For him, there was no child – it was only Grace's child. There was nothing of him.

Silence.

PATRICIA: How do I bear to look at him again? How do I carry on?

BEAUTY: It is what people are doing every day.

PATRICIA: It is what you have done.

BEAUTY says nothing.

PATRICIA: When we get to Durban tomorrow, he must go. I will put him in a home.

BEAUTY: A home?

PATRICIA: For people who are sick.

Silence.

BEAUTY: Must I take him his tea?

PATRICIA: No – not tonight.

BEAUTY: I have remembered his pills.

PATRICIA: Thank you, Beauty.

Silence.

PATRICIA: The sea. Have you ever seen it, Beauty?

BEAUTY: Cha, Mesis.

PATRICIA: Well, tomorrow you will.

Silence.

BEAUTY: That is all, Mesis?

PATRICIA: Yes, Beauty. That is all.

BEAUTY bobs and leaves.

The light fades around PATRICIA.

The End.

THE GIRL IN THE YELLOW DRESS

Production History

The Girl in the Yellow Dress was a co-production between the Market Theatre (Johannesburg), Live Theatre (Newcastle) and the Citizens Theatre (Glasgow).

It was first performed at the Grahamstown Festival on 21 June 2010. It then transferred to the Baxter Theatre in Cape Town, the Traverse in Edinburgh, Live Theatre in Newcastle, the Citizens in Glasgow, the Stadsteater in Stockholm and the Market Theatre in Johannesburg.

A new UK production opened at the Salberg Studio at Salisbury Playhouse on 3 October 2011. The production transferred to Theatre503 in London, opening on 20 March 2012 with the same cast. Several minor text changes, inspired by the Salisbury production, have been made to this edition of *The Girl in the Yellow Dress*.

Since then, there have been other productions of the play in the United States and Britain.

For the Market Theatre production:

Cast

CELIA	Marianne Oldham
PIERRE	Nat Ramabulana

Production Team

Director	Malcolm Purkey
Designer	Gary McCann
Lighting	Nomvula Molepo
Producer	Tshiamo Mokgadi
Production Manager	Drummond Orr
Stage Manager	Emelda Khola

For the Salisbury Theatre production:

Cast

CELIA	Fiona Button
RICHARD	Clifford Samuel

Production Team

Director	Tim Roseman
Designer	James Perkins
Lighting Designer	Dave Marsh
Sound & Projection	Alex Twiselton

Characters

CELIA

PIERRE

The action takes place in contemporary Paris.
There is no interval.

Part One

THE PASSIVE

CELIA's apartment. Her sitting-room is modern and impeccable, giving a suggestion of wealth. The bookshelves are filled with books. On a mantelpiece, there's a vase filled with daffodils. A half-visible kitchen adjoins the sitting-room. There are also entrances from the front door and CELIA's bedroom.

CELIA's mobile phone is on a glass table. It buzzes like an angry bee.

CELIA emerges from the bedroom. She has just had a shower and is still getting ready. Perhaps she is brushing her hair. She is in her late twenties, pale and beautiful.

She ignores the phone and moves through to the kitchen area to prepare a coffee tray. The phone stops buzzing. Then it beeps.

The doorbell rings. CELIA goes to the door.

CELIA: Hello?

PIERRE: Hello.

CELIA: Are you Pierre?

PIERRE: I am him.

CELIA: Then you'd better come in.

> *PIERRE enters. He is French-speaking. Of African heritage. About twenty. He has dreadlocks and wears a dark blue polar neck jumper. While CELIA closes the door behind him, he regards the books.*

CELIA: Would you like to take off your coat?

PIERRE: Thank you.

He removes his coat and hands it to her. She hangs it up by the door.

CELIA: I hope you drink coffee.

PIERRE: Yes.

She moves through to fetch the coffee tray.

PIERRE: It's generous of you to see me.

CELIA: It's what I do.

PIERRE is gazing around surreptitiously. He sees CELIA's row of notebooks on the shelf.

PIERRE: What's the name of this yellow flower, *la jonquille – en anglais* (the daffodil – in English)?

CELIA: Daffodils.

He smells them, but they have no smell.

PIERRE: Daffodils –

CELIA enters with the tray – on which is a cloth, two small, glazed mugs, a bowl of sugar and the coffee. Each object is beautiful, selected with care. She sets the tray down.

CELIA: Please make yourself at home.

PIERRE: At home?

CELIA: Take a seat.

PIERRE: Make myself at home. This is a way of saying please sit?

CELIA: It's a way of saying please relax.

He sits in an armchair at a right angle to the couch.

CELIA: So you're Pierre. You were very insistent on the phone.

PIERRE: Yes.

CELIA: Celia.

She offers her hand. He takes it and holds it.

PIERRE: I know.

CELIA: Pleased to meet you in the flesh.

PIERRE: Pleased to meet you. In the flesh.

CELIA: You look familiar. Haven't I seen you somewhere before?

PIERRE: I don't – perhaps.

She withdraws her hand, flushing slightly.

PIERRE: I have the money.

He tries to give her a few notes.

CELIA: Not now.

PIERRE: I must pay you every time, yes?

CELIA: I prefer it that way.

PIERRE: At the end?

CELIA: Yes.

PIERRE pockets his money.

PIERRE: You think once a week is enough?

CELIA: It's what we agreed to, isn't it?

PIERRE: Every Wednesday morning. Ten o'clock. For one hour and a half.

CELIA: Can you afford that?

PIERRE: Why not? You think I look too – what?

CELIA: I didn't mean anything by it.

PIERRE: I saved up.

CELIA: Well, let's see how we get along. If you're quick, perhaps we can meet a couple of times a week. For shorter periods.

PIERRE: I will like it.

CELIA: Would, not will. We're still being hypothetical.

Silence.

PIERRE: These books. They are impressive.

CELIA: Books are not in themselves impressive.

PIERRE: I mean you. To read these.

Silence.

PIERRE: And you always work from home?

CELIA: I try to. Although I've been cutting down on my working hours.

PIERRE: You said this in the phone.

CELIA: I'd decided not to take on anyone new. But you wouldn't take no for an answer.

PIERRE: No.

CELIA: There are several other places in Paris you could have gone. Why me?

PIERRE: You were recommended by one of the other students at the Sorbonne.

CELIA: I suppose you saw one of my notices. I didn't know they were still up.

PIERRE: They aren't.

Silence.

PIERRE: I kept your number with me. As I'm saying – I had to save up.

CELIA: I was a student there too. For a bit.

PIERRE: Why have you left?

CELIA: It's the past simple, not the past perfect.

PIERRE: Why did you leave?

CELIA: I was doing *le cours de lange et civilisation* (the course in language and civilisation). The course ended.

Silence.

CELIA: Actually, I dropped out. I didn't feel comfortable – trying to be a student again. I'd rather read the books by myself. Form my own opinions.

PIERRE: I know what you mean.

Silence.

PIERRE: You live alone?

CELIA: You ask a lot of questions, Pierre.

PIERRE: Sorry.

CELIA: Shall I pour?

PIERRE: What is 'pour'?

CELIA: Pour the coffee.

PIERRE: Pour the coffee. Yes.

She pours the coffee. PIERRE is watching her every move.

CELIA: There we go.

She passes his coffee. He doesn't take sugar.

PIERRE: Thank you.

She glances at her watch.

CELIA: I suppose we'd better get on with it. You seem fairly proficient.

PIERRE: I do?

CELIA: Have you taken English courses before?

PIERRE: In Dijon. At 'Language Works'. After I finished school.

CELIA: So you know the terminology. The passive, the different tenses and conditionals. Modal verbs and subjunctives. And so on?

PIERRE: Some I maybe had forgotten.

CELIA: We'll need to revise your perfect tenses.

PIERRE: You will see that I learn quickly.

CELIA: Oh, I will, will I?

They regard each other intently – with a strange familiarity.

CELIA: So, Pierre. What are you hoping to get out of this?

PIERRE: I wanted you –

CELIA: Yes?

PIERRE: I thought: you will be the person to help me.

CELIA: Would. With what?

PIERRE: Everything. You would help me to – fit.

CELIA: Into what?

PIERRE: What is there. Around. Ahead.

Silence.

CELIA: I think you overestimate me.

PIERRE: And I want to express.

CELIA: What?

PIERRE: Myself.

CELIA: The verb 'to express' is a transitive verb. It takes an object. You have to express some thing. And the thing you cannot express is yourself?

PIERRE: I can't reveal myself. Through the words. The English words.

CELIA: Do you think any of us can do that?

PIERRE: Some better than the others.

CELIA: Words are better at misleading than revealing, in my experience. But you say you want to express yourself. To something. You have to have an object in mind. What is your object? To whom would you like to express yourself?

PIERRE: You are my object.

CELIA: For now, perhaps.

PIERRE: It's why I came.

CELIA: To be able to express yourself to an English person? In English?

PIERRE: If you like.

CELIA: Why English?

PIERRE: You mean – why not an African language? Swahili, or something like this?

CELIA: Something like 'that'. Swahili isn't here – it's out there, far away somewhere.

PIERRE: English is the language of the world. If you can speak it, you can live or work anywhere. Swahili? You know there's no point of 'that'.

CELIA: How are your listening skills?

PIERRE: I can read and listen. The speaking and the writing are more difficult.

CELIA: Those are the more generative skills. Listening and reading are more passive.

PIERRE: Yes.

CELIA: Perhaps we should consider the passive itself. It's a good test of a person's proficiency. You remember the basic model for the passive?

PIERRE: We use the past participle, I think.

CELIA: It's the verb 'to be' in whatever tense is necessary, plus the past participle.

PIERRE: The verb to be plus the past participle.

CELIA: Could you give me an example?

PIERRE: I was born?

CELIA: Yes. Because you can't give birth to yourself, can you? You rely on someone else for that. Another?

PIERRE: I am taught by you.

CELIA: That's right. Although you're 'being' taught by me, aren't you? It's happening now. The present continuous passive.

PIERRE: The passive in the present continuous.

CELIA: Let's start with something about yourself. What are you doing at the moment?

Silence.

PIERRE: I study the History of the Art.

CELIA: Present continuous. I am studying History of Art.

PIERRE: I am studying History of Art at the Sorbonne. And Western Philosophy. I do a course in Aristotle. Epicurius. Montaigne. Spinoza. John Stuart Mill.

CELIA: Has John Stuart Mill helped?

PIERRE: We haven't arrived at him yet.

CELIA: Reached. Do you paint?

PIERRE: I copy illustrations – *a l'aquarelle* (with watercolours)?

CELIA: With watercolours.

PIERRE: It's something I arrive to do when I am feeling – *pensif* (thoughtful/ sad).

CELIA: You needn't arrive. Although I know the French have to, even when they're already there. Perhaps it's why they're almost always late. The being there is not so important.

PIERRE: Was I late?

CELIA: No, Pierre. I was joking. An English joke. About the French.

PIERRE: Ah.

Silence.

CELIA: Humour has never been my strong point.

Silence.

CELIA: Although you were late. By about six minutes.

PIERRE: I was here for half an hour. Before. Waiting.

CELIA: And yet you were still six minutes late?

PIERRE: I went around the bend. For a walk. Then I came back.

Silence.

CELIA: Right. So – copying copies of other things. This is
    something you 'arrive to do' when you're feeling *pensif*?

PIERRE: Yes.

CELIA: Are you often sad?

PIERRE: No.

CELIA: Is that why you're not a 'proper' artist? Too much
    happiness?

PIERRE: No one is filled with too much happiness. But some
    unhappiness. It is normal, no?

CELIA: A degree of unhappiness is probably normal. I wouldn't
    know. Where did you grow up? Paris?

PIERRE: No.

CELIA: Well, where did you go to school?

PIERRE: In a village near Beaune. I went to school at a place
    named Seurre.

CELIA: You grew up in Seurre?

PIERRE: No.

CELIA: Are you finding this too boring to speak about? Would you rather talk about something else?

PIERRE: No.

CELIA: No?

PIERRE: No.

CELIA: Come on, Pierre. Express something. Surprise me. You aren't here to say 'no' to everything.

PIERRE: It's – difficult.

CELIA: It's what people expect. We have to learn to make up stories about ourselves. To represent ourselves.

PIERRE: Why?

CELIA: I suppose people want to see if your story fits into theirs.

PIERRE: You want me to make up the story?

CELIA: If you like. The actual facts are not always that important. It's how we present the facts that matters more. It's not important that my story is half fantasy. Something I want to be rather than what I am. My imagined parts, you see – they tell you something else. Something that might signify more. My desire. What I want. What I want to move towards. A sense of a future. We want to know that we share a similar sense of a future. The past can become – less significant. Are you following all this?

PIERRE: *(Lying.)* Yes.

Silence.

PIERRE: I have not thought about how to explain myself. In a story. Even in French.

CELIA: Let's begin at a beginning then. Tell me where you grew up.

PIERRE: In a small village next to Seurre. Pouilly-sur-Saone. Our house is on the *bord* (embankment) of the River Saone. This is where I have most of my childhood.

CELIA: Remember – it's far away. And you've already had your childhood.

PIERRE: That was where I had my childhood.

CELIA: Good. Although we usually spend our childhood. Like money. Something precious that's used up. Carry on.

PIERRE: About Pouilly? There's little to tell. It's a small place. Typical of the Bourgogne. One *boulangerie* (bakery), owned by a woman who hates all people and never smiles. Her husband runs the *tabac* (tobacconist).

CELIA: Tobacconist.

PIERRE: The husband also hates, but only his wife. Then there's the post office, with the diamond patterns on the roof. By the church, there's the monument for all the men who died in the war. The wars.

CELIA: Was it dull?

PIERRE: Not dull. It's very colourful in the summer. Of course, there's the River Saone.

CELIA: Tell me about the river.

PIERRE: It's wide, yes? My bedroom sits in the roof of the house. *Dans la mansarde* (in the attic).

CELIA: Attic.

PIERRE: When I open my window, I see the *tilleul* (lime) trees. Huge and soft. The river all below me. When I was younger, I had this yellow kayak that I liked to paddle. In the summer the river is warm, so you can swim.

CELIA: And in the winter?

PIERRE: The water grows high. It 'pours' out on the other side. From my bedroom window, it's like I am living on the side of a long lake, without an end, floating.

CELIA: A country boy. Altogether *provençal* (of the provinces). Do you have brothers, sisters?

PIERRE: There's only me.

CELIA: So what was it like – arriving in Paris?

PIERRE: Fine.

CELIA: Don't you miss your home?

PIERRE: Sometimes. This is when I'm feeling sad.

CELIA: Are you feeling sad now?

PIERRE: No.

CELIA: Then use the present simple.

PIERRE: Sorry.

CELIA: But when you're feeling sad, you copy things. What do you copy?

PIERRE: I copy pictures of the birds. The birds of Pouilly.

CELIA: Tell me about the birds.

PIERRE: I like to watch them during the day. *Les martin-pecheurs.* The little blue fishing birds.

CELIA: Kingfishers.

PIERRE: *Et les rossignols* in the evenings. These are the nightingales. These I know the name for. Sometimes there are five or ten or fifteen of the nightingales singing in the same time. When it's spring, like now, they are singing all in the one time. I imitate them. I make the sound of many birds. Sometimes, they will answer me.

CELIA: They all sing. A general rule. Present simple. What else?

PIERRE*: Les guêpiers.*

CELIA: Wasps?

PIERRE: Bees. Bee-eaters, I think.

CELIA shrugs.

PIERRE: These birds are bright as jewels. They are all the way from Africa during the summer. They nest in the river cliffs.

CELIA: All the way from Africa?

PIERRE: Yes.

Silence.

CELIA: It sounds a bit too perfect, Pierre. Is that all there is to you? A kayak and some nightingales?

PIERRE: What do you desire me to say?

CELIA: I want you to express yourself. Risk something. Tell me a story you're a bit embarrassed about. We only learn to speak fully in a language when we've found something – electric to express. You can say anything. As I say, it doesn't even have to be literally true.

Silence.

CELIA: Would you like more coffee?

PIERRE: No, thank you.

Silence.

CELIA: Surely you have a girl you care about?

PIERRE: No.

Silence.

PIERRE: Yes.

CELIA: Which?

PIERRE: Yes.

CELIA: A girlfriend?

PIERRE: I do not have a girlfriend at the moment.

CELIA: Really?

PIERRE: I have a girlfriend during two years. Back in Pouilly. Elodie. No girlfriend now.

CELIA: For two years? What you mean is that you had a girlfriend. Elodie. For two years. It was a fixed period of time. But now it's finished. Yes?

PIERRE: It's finished. I have a girlfriend for two years.

CELIA: Had a girlfriend. You had her. But the relationship is over. It's gone.

PIERRE: Yes – gone.

Silence.

PIERRE: I never loved her.

CELIA: I think you did. Otherwise you wouldn't say it like that.

PIERRE: Now I love someone else.

CELIA: Oh. And who's that?

PIERRE: She doesn't know.

CELIA: Is she seeing someone else?

PIERRE: I think she's alone.

CELIA: Perhaps you should tell her.

PIERRE: I don't know how to express it.

CELIA: Of course you do. You simply say the words 'I love you'. The words will go as far as words can go in expressing it. Whatever 'it' is.

PIERRE: She doesn't know me so well.

CELIA: In time, she can get to know you better.

PIERRE: She has only seen me the once.

CELIA: Then you must try to see her 'the twice'.

PIERRE: I will.

Silence.

CELIA: But how can you know?

PIERRE: Know?

CELIA: How can you be in love with her when you've only
seen her once?

PIERRE: I've seen her many times. It's that she doesn't see me.

CELIA: What do you mean?

PIERRE: She lives in the same street as I do. La rue St-Jacques.
At the other side of the city. I see her in the supermarket,
choosing the cheese. At the bookshop, buying the books.
I've even walked behind her in the *Jardin du Luxembourg*
(Luxembourg Gardens).

CELIA: I see.

PIERRE: I've discovered many things about her.

CELIA: Like what cheese she chooses?

PIERRE: Yes.

CELIA: You follow her about?

PIERRE: No, no – or not for long.

CELIA regards him.

CELIA: How do you know that you even like this woman?
It's clearly more about you than her. Alright, you know she
buys Comté instead of Emmenthal –

PIERRE: Manchego, actually – the sheep's milk cheese from
Spain.

CELIA: Right. But I'm sure many people buy that.

PIERRE: I also see the way she smiles. She can hold her head to the one side – as if she's listening to something I can't hear.

CELIA: She's just anyone.

PIERRE: No, she isn't.

CELIA: She's probably a nutcase.

PIERRE: She's the one I was waiting for.

CELIA: Have been waiting for. It continues into the present, doesn't it?

PIERRE: Yes.

Silence.

CELIA: My advice is that you leave her alone. When you project your desires onto other people, you can only disappoint yourself.

Silence.

PIERRE: The coffee. Please. I will have it now. I change my mind.

CELIA: Have changed it. You changed your mind, but we don't know exactly when.

She takes the coffee through to the kitchen area and switches on the kettle.

PIERRE: You're right. There is more to me than – the nightingales.

During the following, PIERRE stands – he goes over to the bookshelves where CELIA keeps her notebooks in a row. CELIA is occupied in the kitchen area.

CELIA: Oh yes?

PIERRE: I want to tell you everything.

CELIA: Well, it needn't be everything.

PIERRE: I know you are wanting to help.

CELIA: I want to help. A general fact. Not something I am only doing in the present. As a temporary activity.

PIERRE: The present simple – yes.

PIERRE takes out one of the notebooks. He hears CELIA coming and doesn't have time to put it back. He hides it behind his back.

CELIA enters. PIERRE stuffs the notebook into his trousers behind his back.

CELIA: What was it?

PIERRE: What?

CELIA: What did you want to say?

Silence.

PIERRE: I am from Africa.

CELIA: Like those – wasp birds?

PIERRE: *Oui, comme les guêpiers* (Yes, like the bee-eaters)?

CELIA: Did something bad happen to you. There in Africa?

PIERRE: Something bad happens to many people – there in Africa.

CELIA: Well, I wouldn't be put off. I'm a good listener. My brother used to call me his agony aunt. He said I take a deep delight in the dark side. It was a joke, of course. Another English joke.

PIERRE: Of course.

CELIA: My mother has spent a lot of time in Africa. She's a journalist. You know the *Guardian* newspaper?

PIERRE: *(Lying.)* Yes.

CELIA: She went all over the continent. Ethiopia, Zimbabwe, Rwanda. She loved it there. Where's your family from originally? Is it somewhere – conflicted?

PIERRE: Something like that.

CELIA: Good. I mean, it's good that you said 'that' and not 'this'. I didn't mean –

Silence.

PIERRE: I think I need time to – think. About my story. In English. Can I prepare it for another time?

CELIA: If you like. It might be better to call it a day. I mean for today.

PIERRE: Please – no.

CELIA: I needn't charge you. This can be an introductory session. A getting to know each other. Before the actual start.

PIERRE: I want to continue with this lesson. Not call it a day. I must continue with practicing the passive.

The kettle is boiling in the kitchen.

Blackout.

Part Two

NARRATIVE TENSES

CELIA's apartment. There is thunder outside. Rain. CELIA is pouring fresh water into the daffodils when the phone rings.

She picks up the phone.

CELIA: *Allô?* (Hello)?

Silence.

CELIA: Oh hello, Mum.

Silence.

CELIA: He does?

Silence.

CELIA: Can't he pick up the phone and tell me himself?

Silence.

CELIA: So what's the big news?

Silence.

CELIA: He's getting – ? No!

Silence.

CELIA: To whom?

Silence.

CELIA: I see.

Silence.

CELIA: I can't talk about this right now, Mum. I have a student waiting in the sitting-room.

Silence.

CELIA: A boy.

Silence.

CELIA: He's extremely attractive.

Silence.

CELIA: Oh Mum – really. Bye.

She hangs up. On the table are a banana, a knife and a plate. She sits and cuts the banana in half. She starts to eat one of the halves. She stares ahead for a long time. Tears are streaming down her face.

The doorbell rings. She wipes her eyes and goes to answer the door.

PIERRE enters. There is no evidence that CELIA has been upset.

PIERRE: Hello.

CELIA: Is it still raining outside?

PIERRE: It is.

CELIA: Your hair is sparkling.

PIERRE: Sparkling?

CELIA: Glittering. Like there are little stars inside it.

PIERRE: There are stars inside my hair?

CELIA: Yes.

Silence.

CELIA: Come in.

PIERRE: I will make myself at home.

CELIA: You have to be invited to do that.

PIERRE: Invited to relax?

CELIA: I suppose the expression means that you can behave as you do at home. Not stand on formality.

PIERRE: How 'stand on' formality?

CELIA: It means that you can sit, I suppose – put your feet up. Though not literally, of course.

PIERRE is thoroughly confused.

PIERRE: *Les anglais!* (The English!)

CELIA goes through to the kitchen area to fetch the coffee tray – the coffee has been made already. There are two ginger biscuits on a plate – and the same small mugs.

PIERRE has CELIA's notebook. He's about to take it out to return it to the shelves when CELIA enters.

CELIA: Black. No sugar.

PIERRE: You remember.

CELIA: Absolutely everything.

They sit and take a moment to watch the rain outside. Then CELIA pours his coffee. Her hands are shaking slightly. She spills the coffee.

CELIA: Damn.

She takes the cloth from the tray and cleans up the coffee.

CELIA: I don't know what's got into me today.

PIERRE: You have cold?

CELIA: You say 'Are you cold?' when you want to know if someone's cold, and 'Do you have a cold?' if you think someone's ill.

PIERRE: Are you cold?

CELIA: No.

PIERRE: Do you have cold?

CELIA: A cold. No.

PIERRE: Then why do you shake your hands?

CELIA: I don't shake them. They are simply shaking themselves. Perhaps it's my blood sugar. I have problems with that. But we use the present continuous. Because they are shaking now. If I say my hands shake, we are using the present simple and talking about a general habit or situation. And my hands, they don't shake all the time. They don't shake generally.

PIERRE: The present continuous. I remember that.

CELIA: You *will* remember it. In the future. Future simple.

She passes him the coffee.

PIERRE: You do this every time? With every student?

CELIA: Sorry?

PIERRE: Drink coffee. Eat the biscuits.

CELIA: Sometimes. If people live across the river, I can agree to meet them half way. At a cafe. I usually take the bus to the Louvre. I have one student I meet near the Musée Rodin. He's rather ancient. Italian. Monsieur Levi. He once said something – odd. I can only be happy as long as I do not know myself.

Silence.

CELIA: Ignorance is bliss. You know the expression?

PIERRE: *(Lying.)* Yes.

CELIA: You have been to the Musée, of course?

PIERRE: No, never.

CELIA: No wonder you're not a proper artist! It's one of my favourite places in Paris. The house where Rodin lived, the gardens running all around it. It's the small marble works I love the most. They look as though they're made of wax. They glow. I suppose they absorb the light around them somehow. Is that how it works?

PIERRE: I don't know.

CELIA: 'The Centuaress' – the body of the woman melding into the body of a beast.

Silence.

CELIA: You can buy a season ticket for the gardens. We could have the lessons there if you liked.

PIERRE: I prefer it here.

He sips the coffee.

CELIA: Is it how you like it?

PIERRE: It is perfect.

CELIA: Ginger biscuit?

PIERRE: Thanks.

He takes a biscuit.

CELIA: *(Rather proud.)* That's my breakfast.

PIERRE: A biscuit is what you have for the breakfast?

CELIA: And half a banana. Yes.

They gaze at the other half of the banana still on the table.

CELIA: You can have it if you like.

PIERRE: Thanks.

He picks up the remaining half of the banana and eats it. She watches him closely.

CELIA: I never have anything else for breakfast.

Silence – PIERRE eating.

CELIA: So our grammar point for the day is narrative tenses.

He says nothing.

CELIA: Past simple, past continuous, past perfect. You know these terms?

PIERRE: I know.

CELIA: I'd like you to describe a day using the past tenses. It can be any kind of day. A happy day, a sad day, a boring day, a perfect day. But remember: we mainly narrate stories in the past simple.

PIERRE considers.

PIERRE: I describe a happy day.

CELIA: Will describe. Future simple. Okay.

PIERRE: When I wake. Sorry. Woke.

CELIA: Up. You woke up. A modal verb in the past simple. Yes?

PIERRE: When I woke up, I stretched myself with my arms wide and – got out of my bed.

CELIA: Had you slept well? It's an event even further back in time from the series of events being described, so it takes the past perfect tense.

PIERRE: I had slept well.

CELIA: Good.

PIERRE: I had dreamed a dream.

CELIA: You had dreamt it. What was it about?

Silence.

PIERRE: A girl. I had dreamt a beautiful girl.

CELIA: I see. Go on. You got out of bed?

PIERRE: I got out of bed. I went to the shower. I turned it on and stood under the water and I washed me.

CELIA: Myself.

PIERRE: Myself. Then I finished and I dried 'myself' with the towel.

CELIA: What colour is your towel?

PIERRE: It is a blue towel.

CELIA: What kind of blue?

PIERRE: Dark blue.

CELIA: What kind of dark blue?

PIERRE: Like the night.

CELIA: Go on.

PIERRE: Then I go to my bedroom and open my cupboard.

CELIA: So you opened your cupboard.

PIERRE: I opened my cupboard and took my clothes.

CELIA: Describe your clothes.

PIERRE: I took a green T-shirt. And a jean. A pair of jean.

CELIA: Jeans.

PIERRE: And my pullover, what is dark blue. Also like the night. And my socks.

Silence.

CELIA: The clothes you're wearing now. Your happy day is today?

PIERRE: Yes.

CELIA: Go on. What else?

PIERRE: Also I took my – what must I say for it?

CELIA: What?

PIERRE: *Mon slip*. My boxing shorts.

CELIA: Boxer shorts. Underpants.

PIERRE: Underpants.

CELIA: And what colour are those?

PIERRE: Blue. Those are blue.

CELIA: Like the night?

PIERRE: Like the day.

Silence.

CELIA: And what did you do then?

PIERRE: I dressed me – myself – and I left my room.

CELIA: Was the sun shining?

PIERRE: No. The rain was raining. It was raining. My hair got wet. My hair was – sprinkling?

CELIA: Sparkling.

PIERRE: Sparkling.

CELIA: And then?

He looks at her directly.

PIERRE: Then I went to the Metro. I catch the train to Lamarck Caulaincourt. Caught. I caught it. I get out the train and I take the lift up. Then I enter the light and go down the stairs, past that café where I like to go – Le Refuge.

CELIA: I like to go there too!

PIERRE: You do? And so I come here.

CELIA: Yes, you came. And it was still raining.

PIERRE: It was still raining. And when you arrived at the door and saw me, you said to me that I have stars inside my hair.

CELIA: I did. You do. And then what happened?

PIERRE: I am not sure.

The phone buzzes. They do not move. CELIA glares at it.

PIERRE: I do not mind. Please take it.

She picks up the phone and answers.

CELIA: *Allô?*

She goes through to the bedroom.

CELIA: *Monsieur Levi? Je vais venir cet après-midi. Est-ce que ça va?*
(Hello. Mr Levi? I will come this afternoon. Is that okay?)

*PIERRE takes out the notebook he took during the previous lesson.
He goes over to the bookshelves to replace the notebook – and is still
doing so when CELIA re-enters and sees him.*

CELIA: *(Still on the phone.) Merci, monsieur. Au revoir.* (Thanks.
Goodbye.) What are you doing, Pierre?

PIERRE: I was looking at a book.

CELIA: Why?

PIERRE: I thought it was a workbook. With lessons inside.

CELIA: I don't believe that. You were prying through my
private things.

PIERRE: What is prying?

CELIA: You know exactly what it means. What do you want?

PIERRE: What?

CELIA: What have you come here for?

PIERRE: English lessons.

CELIA: There's some other thing going on here that I'm not
even aware about, isn't there?

PIERRE: Maybe. It's nothing – bad.

CELIA: I have no idea who you are.

Silence.

PIERRE: Listen, I'm sorry I go through your stuff – went. I don't
mean to be prying.

CELIA: It's something you did by mistake, is that it?

PIERRE: No, I was – uneasy.

CELIA: Well, you're not the only one. The way you come in here and look at everything. The way you look at me. Not as a student. Not as you should – were you polite. It makes me profoundly uneasy.

PIERRE: Why, because I'm black?

CELIA: What? That's absolutely not what I'm talking about.

PIERRE: Isn't it? I think it's the exact thing we're talking about. Can I afford to pay? Why aren't I learning Swahali?

CELIA: I never even said that! You said that!

PIERRE: I'm the one from the heart of darkness, yes?

CELIA: Pierre, for God's sake!

PIERRE: Don't worry. I've read that book. The cannibals that come out of the bush. The forest of heads on the sticks, all along the river. Open your books to page number twenty six! And me – the only dark one there!

CELIA: I don't know what you're going on about. This has nothing to do with race – it's about mutual respect!

PIERRE: Exactly! You pretend you want to help. You act all nice. But deep down you are always thinking – thank God I'm not like him. Always needing help. Thank God I'm civilised!

CELIA: This is – mad!

PIERRE: I know it's mad!

CELIA: You're turning me into something I'm not.

PIERRE: And you aren't doing the same to me?

CELIA: Well, what are you then?

PIERRE: I wish I knew!

Silence.

PIERRE: Whenever I close my eyes and stop, I see them.
Even in the streets of Paris, or coming out the Metro.
Always, I am carrying them in my head.

CELIA: Who?

PIERRE: They come when we are still asleep. Before the sun is
come up.

CELIA: Is this some sort of – dream?

PIERRE: When they look at you, they don't see you. They have
too many ants inside their head.

CELIA: But who are they?

PIERRE: Boys mostly. All of them – blind.

CELIA: I need you to explain yourself.

PIERRE: I know you do.

CELIA: I want to understand!

PIERRE: They are the Interhamwe.

CELIA: The who?

PIERRE: You don't even know who they are!

CELIA: No. Are they phantoms? Spirits? What?

PIERRE: They are like the walking dead – yes. But they carry
guns. Children with guns who kill hundreds every week.
The Interhamwe are the Hutu militias that are coming
from Rwanda.

CELIA: You are saying you're from – Rwanda?

PIERRE: No, the Congo. They ask for money. If you give, they
kill you. If you don't, they kill you. My father's genitals
they cut out and throw them in the yard. My mother and
my sisters they rape.

CELIA: I can't –

PIERRE: Because the sun is not come up, I slip away. Into the bush. Across the old banana plantation.

Silence.

PIERRE: I ran away. I fled. I left them there to die!

CELIA says nothing.

PIERRE: Is that enough darkness for you?

PIERRE is almost weeping with rage and remorse.

PIERRE: Are you satisfied?

Silence.

PIERRE: All the people were killed. Even the dogs. Thrown on a mountain of bodies to be burned.

CELIA: My God.

PIERRE: I was taken by the *medicins sans frontiers* (doctors without borders). I was brought to France. Given to a white family in the Bourgogne. To be adopted. And that – is it. That is how I came to be at Pouilly.

Silence.

CELIA: Why are you telling me all this now?

PIERRE: It's what you want to hear, isn't it?

CELIA: No.

Silence.

CELIA: Yes.

Silence.

PIERRE: When you look at me, it's what you expect.

CELIA's phone starts buzzing. They don't move.

CELIA: I don't know what to expect.

Silence.

PIERRE: Who is this – Oliver?

CELIA: What?

PIERRE: I saw his name. In your book.

CELIA: He's my brother.

PIERRE: He's older than you?

CELIA: Twenty minutes younger.

PIERRE: And where is he now?

CELIA: I really can't talk about it.

> *The phone is still buzzing.*
>
> *Blackout.*

Part Three

CELIA's apartment. Darkness. The phone is still buzzing. It stops.

Light grows. CELIA is on the couch, posing, while PIERRE sketches her.

The phone beeps.

CELIA: Today we are learning about articulating conditions. If you do this, I do that. They're called conditionals.

PIERRE glances at her phone.

PIERRE: Why do you never answer your phone?

CELIA: Have you done your homework?

PIERRE: It's the way you look at it.

CELIA: Have you prepared something?

PIERRE: You think it will bite you?

CELIA: We should probably start with the zero conditional.

PIERRE: Or is there a person who wants to bite?

CELIA: What's the model for the zero conditional?

PIERRE: Present tense plus present tense?

CELIA: Give me an example.

PIERRE: You never say about yourself. You make me say about myself. But you are always asking the questions.

CELIA: I ask the questions because I am teaching you how to speak English. I already know how to speak it.

PIERRE: So when you can speak English, there's no longer a need to talk?

CELIA: My job is to pass on what I know until you can speak for yourself. It's not to tell you about myself.

PIERRE: Then change your job.

CELIA: You should've been content with what you had before you came here.

PIERRE: I want what you have.

CELIA: Oh, and what's that?

PIERRE: The world.

CELIA laughs.

PIERRE: You're beautiful, clever, rich. Most of all, you're white. You can go anywhere, always a bit higher than everything else.

CELIA: That's not a very nice thing to say.

PIERRE: Maybe you don't see it because for you it's normal. Or you do see it, but you don't like it to be said. You don't know what it is to be made always a bit lower than everything. Always – suspicious.

CELIA: The only person who can free you from that feeling is you. There are bigots everywhere – and they'll always pick on something, whoever you are.

PIERRE: You could try to help. By letting me in. By telling about yourself. As an equal. A friend.

CELIA: We're student and teacher. You came here so I could correct your grammar.

PIERRE: That's not why I came.

CELIA: Okay – you wanted to express yourself. Aren't you doing that? Aren't you getting from me exactly what you wanted?

PIERRE: Not exactly.

CELIA: Then what do you want – exactly?

PIERRE: I'll tell you when you're – softer.

CELIA: Listen, I've never been softer in my life.

Silence.

CELIA: Present tense plus present tense. Try to think of an example.

PIERRE: *(Still trying to draw her.)* Keep still. You keep moving your head.

CELIA: Can't you give it a break?

PIERRE: I'm accustomed to drawing birds – not English girls.

CELIA: The zero conditional.

PIERRE: If he gives himself, she will give herself?

CELIA: Is that what you prepared for me? Anyway – you're wrong. You've slipped into the future simple. It should be: if he gives, she gives. But the zero conditional is not very common. Such clear causality is rare.

PIERRE: You're – losing me.

CELIA: The zero conditional is used for things like scientific experiments. Not everyday life. If you heat water to a hundred degrees, it boils. Humans need a greater deal of uncertainty to express themselves. They don't obey the laws of Science.

PIERRE: *(Still drawing.)* Stop moving!

CELIA: I want to see for myself.

She comes over to look at the drawing. He hides it.

PIERRE: Not yet!

She sits.

PIERRE: Look towards the sky.

CELIA: It's called the ceiling.

He continues drawing.

CELIA: What about the model for the first conditional?

PIERRE: Present simple plus future simple? If he likes her, she will like him?

CELIA: Correct, but slightly presumptuous. It could be: if he likes her, she will consider him.

He continues drawing her for a while.

PIERRE: Why do you not want to talk about yourself?

CELIA: Can't you accept that I am what you see? Isn't that enough?

PIERRE: You said we must make up stories to represent ourselves.

CELIA: Well then I'll make it up in the present. With you. As we go along. Why should stories from the past – whether hideous or dull – represent us? Can't we free ourselves from what happened? Or do we always have to drag it along behind us – like some sort of hideous afterbirth? You didn't choose what happened to you. And neither did I.

PIERRE: What happened to you?

CELIA: Nothing.

PIERRE: Then what did you do?

Silence.

PIERRE: Or not do?

Silence.

CELIA: Tell me the model for the second conditional.

PIERRE: Past simple plus – present simple? I can't remember.

She gets up – pretending to walk towards the kitchen.

PIERRE: What are you doing?

She snatches the pad from him.

CELIA: And who is that supposed to be!

PIERRE: Don't you like it?

CELIA: It looks like an illustration from a magazine.

PIERRE picks up her phone.

PIERRE: You have seven missed calls.

CELIA: Give that back!

PIERRE holds out the phone – and they swap the phone and the pad.

CELIA: My mother is the only person who phones me these days. For your information. And Monsieur Levi.

PIERRE: How do I know this Monsieur Levi isn't your lover?

CELIA: He's as blind as a bat.

PIERRE: He doesn't need eyes in order to kiss you.

CELIA: Well, I would have to tear mine out in order to kiss him.

PIERRE: And you have no other students?

CELIA: I told you: my only other student at the moment is you.

PIERRE tears up his sketch of CELIA.

CELIA: Why did you do that?

PIERRE: I must start again.

CELIA: That is such a violent thing to do to me.

PIERRE: You said it wasn't you.

CELIA: Well, it's as close as you could get.

PIERRE: I want to make it look more alive.

CELIA: You mean me – you want me to look more alive.

He starts again.

CELIA: The second conditional is past simple plus future simple. If he wanted to draw her, she would let him.

PIERRE: If he wanted to draw her, she would let him?

CELIA: Yes.

He continues drawing.

CELIA: Don't look at the drawing. Look at me and let your hand move across the page.

He starts again.

CELIA: It's called contour drawing. You don't concern yourself with the page – you only look at the subject. It's supposed to help you to see directly, without interpretation.

He does this for a while.

CELIA: Let's see.

He hands her the drawing. She looks at it and laughs. He looks at it with her.

PIERRE: The eye looks a bit like yours, don't you think?

CELIA: *(Laughing.)* Which bit of this pile of spaghetti are you referring to exactly?

PIERRE: And the way the hair falls – there.

He touches her hair and pushes a strand of it back.

CELIA: You're very sweet, you know that?

PIERRE: If he wanted –

CELIA: What?

PIERRE: The second conditional. If he wanted to –

CELIA: Yes?

PIERRE: Touch her. She would let him?

Silence.

PIERRE: Is that correct?

Silence.

CELIA: Yes. No.

PIERRE: No?

Silence.

PIERRE: Yes?

CELIA: I meant that was the correct use of the second conditional.

PIERRE: Yes?

CELIA: No.

Silence.

CELIA: She would not let him touch her if he wanted to.

PIERRE says nothing.

CELIA: You see, you can swap the clauses around with conditionals. They still work.

Silence.

CELIA: I think we'd better stop – for today.

PIERRE: I am paying for one hour and a half.

CELIA: I don't like being paid for this.

Silence.

PIERRE: You think I don't understand?

CELIA: What?

PIERRE: Everything.

CELIA: How can you – when I don't myself?

PIERRE: Everyone knows everything. But we hide from it.

CELIA: Your English is improving.

She is trembling slightly.

PIERRE: Why are you shaking?

CELIA: That's good. The present continuous.

PIERRE: *C'est pas le moment de me faire un cours d'anglais.* (This is not the moment for an English lesson.)

CELIA: It's exactly the moment for an English lesson.

PIERRE: I want to kiss you.

CELIA: The third conditional. We haven't done it yet. It requires the past perfect and the present perfect with the – the subjunctive. I forget.

PIERRE: If he had touched her, then she might – have wanted it?

CELIA: Yes – something along those lines.

PIERRE touches her face.

CELIA: I grew up in Primrose Hill. With my brother. And my mother. Did I tell you that?

PIERRE: Now you want to talk?

Her whole body is shuddering slightly.

CELIA: We lived in Chalcott Square.

PIERRE: It sounds pretty.

CELIA: We had a Japanese garden at the back. My brother and I had the job of collecting the snails. We would take them to the railway bridge in a bucket and let them go in the willowherb.

PIERRE: How lovely.

CELIA: Are you listening?

PIERRE: You throw the snails in the willowherb.

CELIA: My mother was often away.

PIERRE: Why away?

CELIA: For months at a time. In Africa somewhere. Writing her next book.

PIERRE: Ah yes.

CELIA: She was always a little in love with African men. She said she found them sexy. I think she had several affairs. But she always left them there – where she'd found them.

PIERRE: Very sensible.

CELIA: She'd come back from each trip with gifts for me and Oliver. Dolls made from beads. Carved wooden figures with straw coming out their heads.

PIERRE: *(Ironic.)* Black magic.

CELIA: She'd find you – alluring. And want to know everything about you. She'd probably put you in a book. You know her books have been translated into nine different languages? Perhaps you've read one of them. She's popular throughout Europe.

PIERRE: Are you nervous? Your whole body – it is shaking.

CELIA: My father was a surgeon. I was always a bit – dim. Around him.

PIERRE: Dim?

CELIA: Out of focus as well as stupid. Like we were not where he was. He left when we were about ten.

PIERRE takes her hand.

CELIA: Both my parents are considered a great success. Olly too. I've somehow become the family flop. Sitting here, teaching people like you. It's not what anyone imagined for me. I was supposed to be – exceptional. I was going to be an actress, then a novelist. I won't even manage being a mother at this rate. And as for teaching English –

PIERRE: Celia, I'm not here to learn English.

CELIA: We shouldn't even be doing this.

PIERRE: Because you're my teacher? I'm not a child.

CELIA: Please – don't.

She withdraws her hand.

PIERRE: Alright. I won't touch. But we can speak. Yes?

CELIA: Yes.

PIERRE: Tell me a thing you have never told to anyone.
Something – dangerous. I want to know everything about
you.

CELIA: People say that but they never really mean it.

PIERRE: I gave a secret part of me. Now I want one from you.

They stare at each other.

CELIA: Do you know how to keep your mouth shut?

PIERRE demonstrates how he can keep his mouth shut – and nods.

CELIA: Well, I suppose I could tell you that I take things. Is that
enough?

PIERRE: What do you take?

CELIA: Sometimes things from shops.

PIERRE: What things from shops?

CELIA: Oh, silly things. Nail varnish. Lip balm. A nail file.

PIERRE: Why?

CELIA: I suppose I imagine I'm not worthy.

PIERRE: To buy it?

CELIA: Of buying it for myself. I've never bothered to
understand it. But I take things. From shops and from
places I stay. Mostly from relatives – and from friends.

Usually things they wouldn't even miss. Like a comb, or soap. Sometimes I take a book.

PIERRE: When did it begin?

CELIA: Start. You say start. It started when I was about twelve, thirteen.

Silence.

CELIA: We could talk about it all day and not get to the bottom of it.

PIERRE: Which of these books did you take?

CELIA: That one there. Rilke's poems. I took that from my father's study.

PIERRE: After he left or before?

CELIA: After, of course.

PIERRE: But that's not stealing.

CELIA: I took *Sons and Lovers* from a friend who lives in Surrey. From her parents' house, in fact. I take books whenever I go there. Rebecca's parents is where I got most of my Virginia Woolf. Would you like me to carry on? For a while I worked at a bookshop. I stole a great many books from there. All my Everyman's Library. That entire row.

PIERRE: You must try to stop.

CELIA: I am.

PIERRE: Good.

Silence.

PIERRE: Why do you do it?

CELIA: I suppose I like the thrill. Living with the guilt. Having something I can focus on and feel particularly bad about. I mean bad in a particular sense – rather than just generally.

Silence.

CELIA: Now you – you tell me something.

PIERRE: My secret? But I already have.

CELIA: Another one then.

PIERRE: I – can't think of a small one.

CELIA: Only big ones?

PIERRE: *(Laughing.)* Yes!

Silence.

CELIA: Alright. A big one then.

PIERRE: I have one that is involved with you.

CELIA: Oh yes?

PIERRE: It's that I saw you first wearing a yellow dress.

CELIA: Which yellow dress?

PIERRE: The one that is simple – your arms bare
    (demonstrating) to here – going to the length of your knees.

CELIA: Ah that. Yes – I stole that dress from Le Bon Marché!

PIERRE: Well, you were wearing it when I saw you at the
    Sorbonne, putting up your notices. It was still September
    then. Autumn.

CELIA: Oh.

Silence.

CELIA: When you first came here, you said there was this girl. In
    the Luxembourg Gardens. The girl you were watching. Me?

PIERRE: I used to see you at the Sorbonne.

CELIA: I've never bought sheep's milk cheese from Spain in
    my life.

PIERRE: Well, I made that bit up.

CELIA: I don't even remember going food shopping around there. Why would I? There's a perfectly good place next door.

PIERRE: When I first saw you at the Sorbonne, I took down your number and your address. When you disappeared, I called – but there was no reply.

CELIA: There rarely is!

PIERRE: So I decided to come up here. To see where you live.

CELIA: The psychologists call it scopophilia. It's an illness. There's the pleasure of looking and the pleasure of being looked at. Would you describe yourself as a *voyeur*?

PIERRE: It was seeing you that made me into that.

CELIA: Right, so it's all my fault!

PIERRE: For being beautiful. Yes!

Silence.

CELIA: So you came up here to look at me. What happened next?

PIERRE: You left the apartment and went into the supermarket. I followed you in – and then I turned and left.

CELIA: And you only did this the once?

PIERRE: Maybe the twice.

CELIA: *(Rather pleased, in spite of herself.)* How absolutely hideous.

PIERRE: I know it wasn't right. I wanted to call again. But I had become too – nervous.

CELIA: Not as nervous as I would have been!

PIERRE: I thought: if I can get that English girl to like me, I can be alright.

Silence.

CELIA: Should I be calling the police?

PIERRE: I'm not dangerous.

Silence.

CELIA: When you were watching me. What did I do?

Even PIERRE can sense she's relenting.

PIERRE: Many things. Like brushing your hair by the window. It was longer then. Reading your books at Le Refuge. Walking to the Cimetière de Montmartre – to Truffaut's grave. Buying goat milk cheese and *tartelettes citron* (lemon tarts).

CELIA: I think I should definitely be calling the police!

PIERRE: I followed you up the hill to Montmartre once. You stopped outside Au Lapin Agile and took off your sandals. You went past the grape vines, up through the tourist shops. It was getting dark. Sacré Couer was lit up on the hill. Outside, there were people playing the drums, smoking hashish, kissing – but you went up the stairs and into the church, and sat near the front, staring at the huge Christ in the dome, with his arms spread wide. The altar was made of gold. There was a single nun standing in front of it. She lifted her arms and started to sing. Like an angel. It was as if you were about to step up into heaven. The nun, she lifted her arms again and all the people in the church started to sing.

CELIA: I remember how beautiful it was. It made one imagine there could be a God. I'm not sure I like the idea of you watching me right then.

PIERRE: I could see how alone you looked. Sitting there, so upright, with the drums playing outside. It's why I was finally courageous enough to phone. I thought with you I might have a chance.

CELIA: I should probably be booting you out.

PIERRE: Should you?

CELIA: Somehow, I'm not afraid of you at all. You're about as dotty as me!

PIERRE: You aren't 'dotty'.

CELIA: You have no idea.

Silence.

CELIA: I want to look at your feet.

PIERRE: What?

CELIA: My grandmother always said – you can judge a man by his hands and his feet. I've already seen your hands. Now I want to look at your feet.

PIERRE, amused, takes off his shoes and his socks.

CELIA: So you followed me, did you – with those feet?

PIERRE: With those feet. What do you think?

She touches them, feels his soles.

CELIA: I say 'those'. You say 'these'. Because they belong to you.

PIERRE: They can belong to you if you like.

CELIA: Granny always said: 'Never trust a man with soft hands and feet!'

PIERRE laughs.

PIERRE: In Pouilly my feet were firm, but I'm a Parisian now.

CELIA: A *flâneur* (one who walks around idly), with lovely long toes.

PIERRE: Now yours.

CELIA: My what?

PIERRE: My grandmother said – before you marry a girl, you must look at her feet.

CELIA: Marriage? Let's not get carried away!

She puts out her feet and allows him to remove her shoes for her.

CELIA: There. Those are my feet.

PIERRE: Can I touch them?

CELIA: If you like.

He touches her feet.

CELIA: You must have done this before.

PIERRE: Touched your feet?

CELIA: Been a bit of a stalker. Did you follow that other girlfriend about?

PIERRE: Elodie?

CELIA: The one you pretended not to love.

PIERRE: Yes.

CELIA: Tell me more about her.

PIERRE: But it's your turn to tell a bad thing.

CELIA: This time you go first.

PIERRE: Only if I can touch your feet.

CELIA: If I allow you to touch my feet, you will tell me. Which conditional is that?

PIERRE: The first!

CELIA: You're a clever boy.

Silence.

PIERRE: I am climbing a ladder and seeing a whole new world.

CELIA: Stick to the topic. You were telling me about Elodie.

PIERRE: Okay. It's late at night. And she's with Etienne. There's a streetlamp, lighting the tree they stand under. All around is darkness. And they kiss.

CELIA: And she was your girlfriend at the time – this Elodie?

PIERRE: Oh yes!

CELIA: Go on.

PIERRE: I only watch. I never confront. I follow them all the way back to where Elodie lives. They enter the house and go up to her room, which looks down on the street. I wait there until the light goes out.

CELIA: And were you friendly with this boy she was with?

PIERRE: Etienne was my closest friend!

Silence.

PIERRE: When I saw them together, something inside me broke.

CELIA: Poor Pierre. And you've had no other girlfriend since?

PIERRE: Only a prostitute once in Paris.

CELIA: I really don't want to know about that!

Silence.

PIERRE: I hate Paris.

CELIA: So do I.

PIERRE: It's supposed to be so romantic, but all I see is – dirt. When you have no money, you feel like dirt. But you don't know what I'm talking about. You're rich!

CELIA: Not exactly. But I suppose I can get by with odd jobs – odd jobs like you.

PIERRE: Thanks!

CELIA: There's a family trust. From my mother's side. I
sometimes think it's the worst thing that ever happened to me.

PIERRE: That's because you're rich.

Silence.

PIERRE: Why did you come to live in Paris?

CELIA: To get away, I suppose.

PIERRE: From what?

CELIA: England. London. My family.

PIERRE: Why?

CELIA: I needed a fresh start.

PIERRE: Your mother. She's still going all the time to Africa?

CELIA: No – it's India now. The mysterious East!

PIERRE: And your brother?

CELIA: Oliver?

PIERRE: I thought you were close.

CELIA: A bit too close for comfort.

PIERRE: What is that?

CELIA: Do we need to go into it?

PIERRE: It's your turn to speak.

CELIA: Well, I had to get away from him because – he's sick.

PIERRE: Sick?

CELIA: He has – inappropriate thoughts. What the doctor calls
intrusive thoughts.

PIERRE: Why intrusive?

CELIA: The idea is that the thoughts come from somewhere
else. The outside. They're not his.

PIERRE: Who else's can they be?

CELIA: He wants to disown them. But they keep on intruding. They come when they're least wanted. For reasons of their own.

PIERRE: What does he think exactly?

CELIA: He thinks about doing things.

PIERRE: To who?

CELIA: To whom. He's the subject. I'm the object.

PIERRE: You're the object?

CELIA: Yes.

PIERRE: But what kind of things does he think about?

CELIA: For God's sake! You want me to spell it out?

PIERRE: Yes!

CELIA: He desires me. Alright? He wants to do things to me. At least – that's what the thoughts are. The intruding thoughts. He can't control them, but that's what they represent.

Silence.

CELIA: He's also a good boy. A good person. Not some freak.

PIERRE: Right.

CELIA: He's been destroyed by it. In ruins. It's not what he would have chosen for himself.

PIERRE: It? You mean you.

CELIA: It simply happened. There's nothing he or anyone else can do about it. But the more he worries about it, the more it happens.

PIERRE: I see.

CELIA: So I had to get away. For his own good – and mine. To give us all some peace.

Silence.

PIERRE: Why are you telling me this?

CELIA: Sometimes when I'm with you, it's as if I'm with him. I mean – you couldn't be more different. And I like you – in a totally separate way. But being with you makes me imagine I'm repeating something. Making the same – mistake.

PIERRE: I am not Oliver.

CELIA: And I am not Elodie.

Silence.

PIERRE: You think there can be a chance for us?

CELIA: Could.

PIERRE: Why do you look so afraid?

CELIA: I'm afraid of committing some – deep sin. I don't want to be like my mother.

PIERRE: Lying with a man who looks like one of your voodoo dolls?

CELIA: Just – lying.

PIERRE: Yes, with me.

CELIA: With you. To you. They're simply prepositions.

PIERRE: I love you.

CELIA: I don't know what that means.

PIERRE: I loved you from the moment I saw you at the Sorbonne.

The phone starts to ring.

CELIA: That'll be my mother. She'll want to know if I'm coming to the wedding.

PIERRE: The wedding?

CELIA: Oliver's wedding.

Silence.

CELIA: He doesn't love her. It's another ploy. To make me feel shit.

PIERRE: Don't answer it.

The phone is still buzzing.

CELIA: Thanks for tracking me down.

PIERRE: The girl in the yellow dress!

CELIA: Yes!

They laugh. PIERRE kisses her. She doesn't resist.

Fade to black.

Part Four

LIES AND TRUTH

CELIA's apartment.

CELIA: So sometimes we say. Sometimes we speak. Sometimes we tell. Sometimes we talk. But these verbs are not interchangeable. What do we do with a lie and the truth?

PIERRE: I don't know what you want.

CELIA: Do we say a lie, speak a lie, tell a lie? Which?

PIERRE: I think we tell a lie.

CELIA: And the truth?

PIERRE: We tell the truth.

CELIA: Usually. We try to. And your mind?

PIERRE: You tell your mind.

CELIA: You speak your mind.

PIERRE: Speak your mind.

CELIA: And you talk nonsense and you say what you think. Got that?

PIERRE: You talk nonsense and you say what you think.

CELIA: Let's talk about lying first. There are a number of modal verbs and expressions we could consider. You can live a lie and tell a pack of lies. You can even lie through your teeth. Are you familiar with these?

PIERRE: I think so.

CELIA: To lie through your teeth isn't separable. The object can't come between the verb and the particle. But some modal verbs are always separable. You have to lie your way out of a situation. Here, the modal verb to 'lie out' is broken in half by the phrase 'your way'.

PIERRE: Is 'your way' the object?

CELIA: It's hard to explain. You simply have to learn modal verbs as units of meaning.

PIERRE: You're leaving me behind.

CELIA: For example, there's also the modal verb to 'make out'. You can make out with someone, which is to kiss them, or something – I don't exactly know as it's American. But the verb 'to make' and the particle 'out' do not have anything to do with kissing in themselves. 'Make' and 'out' have two entirely separate meanings from the expression to 'make out'. And the verb to 'make out' is inseparable in this case.

PIERRE: You're going too fast.

CELIA: 'Make out' can also become separable. But its meaning will change. You can say 'he will make an honest woman out of me'. Here, 'an honest woman' is the object, which comes in the middle of the modal verb – and the verb and particle 'make' and 'out' have entirely new meanings. As I say, you must learn these as units. In isolation. Don't try to analyse them. For logic. There is no logic. There's only learning it. Accepting it as something that already – exists.

Silence.

PIERRE: Are you alright?

CELIA: Absolutely. I'm fine. Sorry. I'll pause.

Silence.

PIERRE: Honesty is the best policy. That's another expression, no?

Silence.

PIERRE: Are we never going to talk about it?

CELIA: What's there to talk about? If there was something to talk about, surely you would have phoned? I waited all week. Silence. Then you arrive here today as if nothing's happened.

PIERRE: Every Wednesday morning. Ten o'clock.

CELIA: What was it? You got what you wanted – and then I no longer mattered?

PIERRE: Of course you mattered.

CELIA: I thought we had a relationship.

PIERRE: We did.

CELIA: You said you loved me.

PIERRE: I did.

Silence.

CELIA: I do hope you're using your tenses deliberately.

Silence.

CELIA: Do you know how insane I went? All week, waiting for you to phone. Every time I went out, I even hoped you were following me again. I stopped at street corners so the imaginary you could catch up.

PIERRE: I don't know why you're blaming me for this.

CELIA: Sorry. Who else should I be blaming? The pope?

PIERRE: I thought you didn't want me.

CELIA: How could you possibly have thought that? I gave myself to you, didn't I? Completely!

PIERRE: It wasn't like that.

CELIA: But we made love! We lay over here – on the floor – and I let you do whatever you wanted. Was that nothing?

PIERRE: I thought it would be – everything.

CELIA: And then it wasn't. You thought I was something else. Something special. Floating a bit above everything. I never asked to be put on some pedestal.

PIERRE: Didn't you?

CELIA: You began despising me the moment I started to like you. You thought: her standards are too low; I can do better than this.

PIERRE: That isn't how it was.

CELIA: You think people are something to climb up. Like ladders! But when will it be enough? At what point will you be able to say – yes, this is me! I'm comfortable inside my own skin!

PIERRE: I wanted to – reflect.

CELIA: What was there to 'reflect' on?

PIERRE: It all seemed so violent. Then afterwards, when you were sick, and told me to get out – what was I supposed to do? I imagined I'd become disgusting to you. But now, when you talk about it, you turn it all around – as if it's my fault.

CELIA: That isn't how it was. We found something together – we reached something, didn't we? I shared myself with you – utterly – as I don't think I've ever done before. I considered it a real accomplishment!

PIERRE: And afterwards you were sick in the toilet.

CELIA: Well, I don't understand that myself.

PIERRE: And you told me to get out.

CELIA: I asked you – I didn't tell. I said I needed a bit of time alone. I only meant for you to go around the block. For a walk. But you never came back. Or called to see if I was alright.

Silence.

CELIA: The fact is, you were disappointed, Pierre. I wasn't what you'd hoped I'd be.

PIERRE: That isn't true.

CELIA: Do you think a woman doesn't know every single thought that goes through a man's head?

Silence.

PIERRE: Maybe I was disappointed. Flat. Like I'd been used up. Playing a part I didn't comprehend. It wasn't me you wanted. It was something else. An idea of someone else.

CELIA: Didn't I shout out your name? Remember how I sobbed in your arms!

PIERRE: I didn't like that. What was there to cry about?

CELIA: God – it was as if a whole lifetime of shame and misery and isolation was being lifted. I'd never been so liberated – and so full of hope!

PIERRE: I'm sorry I didn't experience it like that. I felt – trapped. Trapped in the old way, playing a part I never chose for myself.

CELIA: Right.

Silence.

PIERRE: I'm sorry, Celia.

CELIA: For what?

PIERRE: For all the disappointment.

CELIA: That's far too vast a subject for you to grapple with.

PIERRE: There's no need to insult me.

CELIA: You call that an insult? That's not an insult! That's a little song in the park. You coward. You liar. You insinuating, spineless little boy – stealing biscuits from the biscuit tin and then hiding away. Those are insults.

PIERRE: Why must you speak to me like this?

CELIA: You follow me around, go through my stuff, nose about – like some dog. Then when you get at me at last, and have satisfied yourself, you piss on me and slink off.

PIERRE: I'm not a dog.

CELIA: Aren't you? We make love – and then you leave, without a word. For what? Some other bit of tail to sniff? What's next for you, Pierre? Mandarin? Do you have a pretty little Chinese pug all lined up?

PIERRE: Who are you – to talk to me about love!

CELIA: Why can't I?

PIERRE: You lie there like I'm raping you. All the time shaking. Biting your lips. As if you're waiting for it to be over. Sobbing. Clinging to me – like I'm some dead rock. Trying not to be sick!

CELIA: Oh, stop it!

PIERRE: Then you shout 'come all over me', like it's something disgusting you want to do to yourself. 'Come on my breasts, come all over my mouth!' You cry out like a little girl – all the time using this stupid child's voice.

CELIA: Please stop!

PIERRE: You make me the little boy, stealing biscuits from the tin. But the child – that is you!

CELIA: Please!

PIERRE: You make me like rubbish. A criminal. Rapist! A savage!

CELIA: Well you are a savage, to speak to me like this!

PIERRE: But you are a nothing. Using me to make yourself look good. Without me, you don't even exist!

CELIA: Who taught you to speak to a woman like this?

PIERRE: Oh, be polite! Be polite! What's that about? You
    think I must be treated like an animal, insulted and spat at
    and kicked, and still I must have manners at the end of it?
    What do you expect? You people are all the same!

CELIA: What people is that?

PIERRE: White people!

CELIA: You're the racist – not me!

PIERRE: Black people can't be racists. We're the victims
    remember. We're the objects of racism.

CELIA: And will continue to be the objects as long as you get
    off on being the victims! You think we aren't all fucked up?
    We can all find our reasons to be fucked up.

PIERRE: Tell me – what did he do to you?

CELIA: Who?

PIERRE: You know exactly what I'm talking about!

CELIA: Get out!

PIERRE: Did you have sex? Did he fuck you? Did he come all
    over your face?

CELIA: Get out of my house!

PIERRE: He must have. How else can you explain yourself?

CELIA: Stop it!

PIERRE: Your brother is the rapist. But you make me into him.
    You keep him innocent. 'A good person,' you say. And you
    make me in the wrong. It's easy, isn't it? He's like you.

CELIA: He's nothing like me!

PIERRE: But me – I'm from somewhere else. It's easier to
    make me the animal and make him the good one. You
    want to fuck your brother, but that's too dark – so you
    choose to fuck me. You're like your mother! When you

finish with us, what do you do? We must get out – get out of your houses!

CELIA: My brother is dead!

PIERRE: What?

CELIA: He's dead!

PIERRE: How dead? You said he was getting married!

CELIA: It was his funeral I was talking about – not his wedding.

PIERRE: What madness is this?

CELIA: He killed himself. Last month.

PIERRE: I don't believe you.

CELIA: He cut his wrists.

PIERRE: What?

CELIA: With a silver spoon!

PIERRE: You're playing your games with me.

CELIA: Am I? Perhaps I'm starting to express myself. It's what you wanted, isn't it? To see me for what I am. Well, I'm a liar and a thief. Alright? A murderer and a bitch. Are you satisfied?

PIERRE: No, I'm not satisfied. With you I'll never be satisfied. It's better if I go out and never come back. I don't even know why I come!

CELIA: Came! You came!

Silence.

CELIA: You know what? The thing you hate is not that you didn't enjoy it – it's that you did. You enjoyed pretending to rape me. You were as liberated by being an animal as I was. That's why you ran away. You were afraid of what you'd become.

PIERRE: Of what you wanted me to become.

CELIA: Yes – it was me. I showed you who you really are.

PIERRE: Well, it should be 'It was I' – not 'me'. You were the subject. I was the object.

Silence.

PIERRE: I think I've got as much out of these lessons as I need.

He takes out some money.

PIERRE: What's the expression? For services rendered?

He throws the money at her and walks out.

CELIA: Pierre!

Blackout.

Part Five

DEGREES OF UNCERTAINTY

It is six weeks later. The apartment is empty. It is no longer as neat as it was before. The front door is ajar. The daffodils are dead in their vase.

CELIA enters with a box. She is wearing the yellow dress. She looks pale and exhausted, her hair in disarray. She starts to pack some books in the box.

The phone rings.

CELIA: *Allô?* (Hello?)

> *Silence.*

CELIA: Oh, hi Mum.

> *Silence.*

CELIA: Yes, I'll be there.

> *The doorbell rings. CELIA doesn't move to open it. PIERRE pushes the door open and enters. He has a new, summery look about him.*

CELIA: I have to go. I'm in the middle of a lesson.

> *Silence.*

CELIA: A boy.

Silence. CELIA: He isn't at all attractive.

> *Silence.*

CELIA: You too.

> *She hangs up.*

PIERRE: Hello.

> *CELIA continues packing.*

PIERRE: What's happening?

CELIA: I didn't think you'd come.

PIERRE: Are you leaving?

CELIA: Yes.

PIERRE: Paris?

CELIA: Call it Paris if you like.

PIERRE: I see.

Silence.

PIERRE: Are you still angry with me?

CELIA: Call it angry if you like.

PIERRE: I've been feeling bad. About the way we left it.
I'm glad you summoned me back. You call it 'unfinished
business', not so?

CELIA: I don't think I have the words for it.

CELIA continues packing.

CELIA: You haven't even noticed.

PIERRE: What?

CELIA: I'm wearing the dress. Your yellow dress.

PIERRE: No, you –

He realises she is.

PIERRE: It looks different.

Silence.

CELIA: Perhaps I should have ironed it.

PIERRE: No. It's you who looks different.

CELIA: Thanks!

Silence.

PIERRE: You're still beautiful.

CELIA continues packing her books.

PIERRE: So what did you want? To say goodbye? To shout at me?

Silence.

PIERRE comes towards her, insinuating.

PIERRE: Or is it for something else? I've been missing you.

CELIA: The present perfect continuous. Good.

PIERRE: I went away. Back to Pouilly. I saw my old friend Etienne. The one who kissed Elodie under the tree. I thought I'd hit him – but all we did is stand by the river and share a cigarette. He tells me Elodie has married a middle-aged Belgian. He sells bicycle pumps. I must say – the gods are quick!

CELIA: I'm glad you've put all that behind you.

PIERRE: I can't tell you how much your lessons helped.

CELIA: Your English has certainly improved.

PIERRE: It's not only that. You gave me something. Call it my own tree to stand under. With my own girl.

CELIA: I see. You've met someone new. Does she speak Mandarin?

PIERRE: I haven't met anyone yet. But I am ready. Thanks to you.

CELIA: I'd have thought I would've put you off relationships.

PIERRE: No. *(He tries to joke.)* Only relationships with you!

Silence.

CELIA: You know, it was a cowardly thing to do. To change your number like that. But then you were always a bit – what's the word?

PIERRE: Elusive?

CELIA: Underhand.

Silence.

CELIA: Did it occur to you how I got your number?

PIERRE: I suppose you phoned the Sorbonne.

CELIA: The Post Office.

PIERRE: In Paris?

CELIA: In Pouilly-sur-Saone.

Silence.

CELIA: I spoke to a Madame de la Fontaine, I think it was. She hadn't a clue what I was talking about.

PIERRE: Why did you do that?

CELIA: She was insistent that there were no white families in Pouilly who had adopted a Congolese refugee. But when I described you, it all fell into place. She said she knew you well. She trotted out your parents' number right away.

PIERRE: She had no right!

CELIA: We had an interesting conversation. Your father and I. Would you like to know what he said?

PIERRE: Not really.

CELIA: I always knew something wasn't right. About your story. You simply didn't strike me as a refugee. As someone whose parents and siblings had been murdered, and thrown on a mountain of bodies to be burned. I could see you hadn't suffered. Not properly.

PIERRE: What do you know about what a person suffers?

CELIA: I told your father I was a journalist, wanting to write about refugees who had been adopted by French families. I said I believed he had an adopted son called Pierre.

PIERRE: I can't believe what I'm hearing!

CELIA: He told me that I'd made a mistake. You were his child. Or should I say 'are'?

Silence.

CELIA: He sounded more than a little miffed when I asked if he was white.

PIERRE: Fuck you!

CELIA: He went on to confirm that you were born in France. And had never been adopted. You grew up in Pouilly. In a house by the river. The air thick with nightingales.

Silence.

CELIA: Why did you lie, Pierre? Did you want to make me feel sorry for you?

PIERRE: You have no business doing this!

CELIA: Or were you getting off yet again on being the victim? Cashing in on the suffering of others. What for – to look more appealing? Like a puppy in a shop window!

PIERRE: Who do you think you are?

CELIA: Making up stories like that! Tagging me along!

PIERRE: You told me to make something up. You said it doesn't have to literally be true. So that's what I did. Alright?

CELIA: From the start, all you wanted from me was sex!

PIERRE: I wanted so much more from you than that.
And anyway – it wasn't a lie.

CELIA: What?

PIERRE: It was the truth!

Silence.

PIERRE: And it wasn't.

CELIA: It's little wonder you've never known how to express yourself – explain yourself. You're a mess!

PIERRE: It wasn't me from the Congo, alright? It was my parents.

Silence.

PIERRE: My father's from Lake Kivu, between Rwanda and the Congo. He moved to France when the country became Zaire. When the trouble started, he never went back. My mother – her people were from Butembo. She's the refugee. Those things that happened in the Congo. They would have happened to us, if my father hadn't left. That's the third conditional, isn't it?

CELIA: I – have no idea.

PIERRE: *Maman* (Mother) says I'm the lucky one. She watched her mother being raped and dumped in the river. Her father's genitals they threw in the yard for the dogs to eat.

Silence.

PIERRE: So you see, I was lying and I was not lying.

CELIA: I do see that.

Silence.

PIERRE: She also says, if something bad happens to one person, it happens to all of us. It's not the axe hitting the tree that reaches us, it's the echo.

Silence.

CELIA: I can't say I've ever felt that connection. When an axe hits a tree in the middle of a forest, do you feel it? You simply hear about it, don't you?

PIERRE: In Africa, you feel it. Maybe it's different here in Europe.

Silence.

PIERRE: You see, the trees have memory. Their roots take in the blood of the dead and carry it towards the light. They contain the memory of everything that has passed. When you hit one of the old trees with an axe, you are hitting yourself.

Silence.

CELIA: You really know how to take the wind out of a girl's sails, don't you?

PIERRE: I'm sorry I lied. I suppose I was trying to make myself more – exotic. I thought that's what you expected from me. Desired me to be. I wanted you to notice me – and be moved. To believe there was more to me than the nightingales.

CELIA: Oh, I do.

Silence.

PIERRE: Tell me your brother isn't dead.

CELIA: He isn't dead.

PIERRE: And is that the truth?

CELIA: He's very much alive. Living in Primrose Hill. Around the bend from my mother. And he's suddenly in love, apparently. Deliriously. To a redhead called Sophie.

PIERRE: When's the wedding?

CELIA: Next week. That's one of the reasons I'm leaving. I've finally agreed to go along. My mother tells me they're hiring a tent and having 'a bash' at Kenwood House.

PIERRE: So he's getting – better?

CELIA: Oh, there's nothing wrong with Olly. In fact, he's more than usually pleased with himself. Apparently this Sophie has enormous breasts.

PIERRE: But what about his thoughts?

CELIA: Which thoughts?

PIERRE: The intrusive ones. The ones that come from the outside.

CELIA: Oh those. Those are my thoughts. They come from me. From my inside.

PIERRE: From you?

CELIA: I'm the one who's sick.

Silence.

CELIA: I suppose you think me very strange.

PIERRE: It's one of the things I like about you.

CELIA: Nothing lasts for long, I always tell myself. We're sieves, unable to hold onto a mood, an emotion, even a conviction, for long. Everything that's poured into us dribbles out again. We're simply a place where things pass through, things we don't choose and whose final destination is unknown.

Silence.

PIERRE: When I saw you at the Sorbonne, you looked so perfect. I watched the way you greeted everyone. They all seemed to like you. The English girl passing through, leaving everything glowing slightly.

CELIA laughs bitterly.

PIERRE: I wondered what it would take to get your attention.

CELIA: You were enough to get my attention. As you were. From the moment you walked in with those stars in your hair.

They smile.

PIERRE: Did you tell my father about my lie?

CELIA: I said I must have made a mistake.

PIERRE: Thank you.

CELIA: I liked him. When we spoke.

PIERRE: You did?

CELIA: He wanted me to understand that he had achieved something – you.

Silence.

PIERRE: I don't want to leave you like this.

CELIA: You're leaving me. I'm like this.

CELIA picks up a pile of books and takes them to PIERRE.

CELIA: Here. Some of my favourite books. For you to take. As a gift. To keep up with the English.

She hands them over.

PIERRE: Novels?

He looks through the titles.

PIERRE: I prefer self-improvement books. Biographies. And histories. I can never find the time for stories that are made up. What's the point of that?

CELIA: Maybe we need to play around with the facts a little in order to make them bearable. It's why we dream. When we stop dreaming, we go insane.

PIERRE is still looking through the books.

PIERRE: So these are the ones you stole?

CELIA: Perhaps they're the ones I stole for you.

He laughs.

CELIA: You won't read them, will you?

PIERRE: I might.

CELIA: A thousand years of literacy – look where it's got us!

PIERRE stands.

CELIA: I wasn't very good at it, was I?

PIERRE: The sex?

CELIA: The teaching.

PIERRE: No, you weren't.

Silence.

PIERRE: You were too complicated about it.

CELIA: The teaching?

PIERRE: The sex.

They laugh.

PIERRE: The future tenses. We never got to them. You think there's time for one more lesson before I go?

CELIA: We may, we might. We can, we could. We should, we shall. We would, we will. These are all subjunctives. You can plot them on a graph. Each expresses a degree of uncertainty.

They regard each other.

CELIA: Or certainty.

Blackout.

The End.

THE IMAGINED LAND

Production History

The Imagined Land was first produced by the National Arts Festival, the Auto and General Theatre on the Square (Johannesburg) and the South African State Theatre (Pretoria). It premiered at the NAF Festival on Friday, 3 July 2015, before transferring for a run at the Auto and General Theatre on the Square and the South African State Theatre.

Cast

EDWARD	Nat Ramabulana
EMILY	Janna Ramos-Violante
BRONWYN	Fiona Ramsay

Production Team

Director	Malcolm Purkey
Set and Lighting	Denis Hutchinson
Costumes & Props	Jo Glanville
Producer	Daphne Kuhn

Characters

BRONWYN

EMILY

EDWARD

Present day.
Johannesburg, South Africa.

Part One

BRONWYN's sitting room. Late afternoon. EDWARD is sitting in a chair with a notebook on his knee. There are ferns, comfortable leather armchairs, framed watercolours of birds and landscapes, a worn Persian rug, fresh roses, an old wooden chest – but most of all many books, mainly novels. EDWARD makes notes about his surroundings, looking slightly smug. He is in his early forties and is originally from Zimbabwe. He wears faded cream corduroys, a pale blue shirt, a herringbone tweed jacket and leather boots.

EMILY enters. She's an attractive woman in her early forties with a flustered intellectual air.

EMILY: She says she'll be down in a moment.

EDWARD: Thanks.

They look at each other, smile.

EDWARD: I thought you'd be in New York.

EMILY: Are you unpleasantly surprised?

EDWARD: Far from it. It's lovely to see you again.

EMILY: Is it?

She clasps her hands nervously.

EMILY: What brings you to my mother's house?

EDWARD: Oh – research.

EMILY: So you aren't here to ask for my hand in marriage?

EDWARD: *(Smiling.)* Who knows?

EMILY: It was a memorable night, but we're far too old for that.

EDWARD: Yes, far too old.

They smile.

EDWARD: And what brings you to your mother's house?

EMILY: She's been unwell. And as the students are off –

EDWARD: I'm sorry to hear that. I hope it's nothing serious.

EMILY: Nothing the doctors can't fix.

Silence.

EDWARD: Were you intending to call me?

EMILY: I only landed this morning.

EDWARD: That isn't an answer.

EMILY: Isn't it?

Silence.

EMILY: I hadn't made up my mind.

EDWARD: But you are pleased to see me, I hope?

EMILY: I think I am.

He smiles at her.

EMILY: Yes.

Silence.

EMILY: Can I offer you something to drink?

EDWARD: Some water, perhaps?

EMILY smiles back at him and leaves the room.

Silence.

EDWARD makes more notes.

BRONWYN enters and stands at the door, watching him. She is around seventy, her dyed auburn hair growing grey at the roots. But she is still a commanding presence.

BRONWYN: You are writing?

EDWARD: *(Standing up.)* Sorry – yes!

BRONWYN: A poem, perhaps?

EDWARD: Oh – thoughts.

BRONWYN: Thoughts? That sounds dangerous.

EDWARD: *(Amused.)* It does?

BRONWYN: I've always preferred – imagined lands.

Silence.

EDWARD: These are more emotions I'm trying to – formulate.

BRONWYN: That's different. That's more like a poem.

Silence.

EDWARD: *(Shaking her hand.)* It's good to meet you, Mrs Blackburne.

BRONWYN: Has Emily offered you something to drink?

EDWARD: She's getting me some water. Thanks.

BRONWYN: Water? Is that all you want of us? You could have turned on a tap. Please – take a seat. And put away that notebook. It makes me feel hunted.

They sit.

EDWARD: Mrs Blackburne, I want to thank you for agreeing to seeing me.

BRONWYN: Emily tells me the two of you have already met.

EDWARD: At a conference last year at King's College. Yes. I asked her a question about your work.

BRONWYN: Did she answer it?

EMILY enters with a glass of water. She places it next to EDWARD.

EMILY: I hope you'll excuse me. I'd like to unpack.

EDWARD: Of course.

EDWARD watches her leave the room. BRONWYN observes his interest in her.

BRONWYN: Did you get to know each other well?

EDWARD: We only met once. And it was some months ago.

BRONWYN: Was that all it took?

EDWARD: Sorry?

Silence.

BRONWYN: I should probably apologise in advance. I'm not feeling quite myself at the moment.

EDWARD: Yes, Emily mentioned you have been unwell.

BRONWYN: I have a tumour inside my head. Tomorrow they're going to take it out.

Silence.

BRONWYN: The surgeon looks like that actor – that one with the lazy eye.

EDWARD: Forest Whitaker?

BRONWYN: I forget the name.

Silence.

EDWARD: I'm sure he's very good at his job.

BRONWYN: Few people are, in my experience. But you have to trust them anyway. Not only the brain surgeon but the man who changes your car tyre. Our lives are far more precarious than we like to imagine, Mr – ?

EDWARD: Dr Smith.

BRONWYN: That's right. And what brings you here today, Dr Smith?

EDWARD: Your books.

BRONWYN: Not your books?

EDWARD: I haven't actually written any books.

BRONWYN: But it's why you're here, isn't it? For the books you intend to write?

He shrugs.

BRONWYN: In your email you said you were born in Zimbabwe.

EDWARD: We are compatriots.

BRONWYN: I was actually born in East London. The tenth child in a Catholic family. My father was in the merchant navy. As I was born, a German U-boat bombed my father's ship and killed everyone on board. My mother didn't know what to do, so I was handed over to the nuns. I was about to be adopted by a tobacco farmer in southern Rhodesia, but the nuns didn't want to hand me over to a family that wasn't Catholic. They even hid me away me for a bit.

EDWARD: I have read that story before.

BRONWYN: It's a narrative I like to trot out at interviews. Not that I believe a narrative can ever represent a life. Imagined lands – that is all we are, all we have access to.

EDWARD: Yes, that is a recurring theme in your work. And yet you have spent your whole life trying to represent other lives, and writing narratives about them.

BRONWYN: Imagined lands are not the same as imaginary lands, Dr Smith. I never tried to represent alternative realities. The one around me always sufficed. And even that became increasingly impossible to represent.

EDWARD: You are too modest.

BRONWYN: Too modest? No, I don't think so. But I try to be honest.

Silence.

BRONWYN: Where did you grow up?

EDWARD: The same suburb as Emily. Just around the corner from where you lived, in fact. You see my father was a gardener.

BRONWYN: And yet you found your way to Edinburgh?

EDWARD: I was one of the lucky few.

BRONWYN: Now you're being too modest. It's quite an accomplishment.

EDWARD: I wanted to become a doctor – and do some good. Then I read one of your novels, and then I read another, and by the time I'd read all your books I decided I wanted to study Literature instead. I wrote my PhD on your work.

BRONWYN: You think Africa needs critics more than it needs doctors?

EDWARD: Probably not, but I think I'm better suited to this line of work.

BRONWYN: What was the topic of your thesis?

EDWARD: 'The Dialogic Imagination in the Work of Bronwyn Blackburne.'

BRONWYN: That sounds impressive.

EDWARD: It's a fairly standard way of approaching your work.

BRONWYN: Is it? I long ago stopped reading anything resembling a review.

Silence.

BRONWYN: These days even I find my books impossible to look at. On the few occasions I've peered into their pages, I've been filled with regret.

EDWARD: Regret?

BRONWYN: Each book represents a different kind of failure. You put the best of yourself into each of them – that bit of gold dust you're given each new day – but when they come out the world simply carries on. As Auden said: poetry makes nothing happen.

EDWARD: But your books have travelled the world. Spoken to thousands of people you will never meet, in languages you will never know. It's impossible to measure what effect they might have had out there. They changed my life, for a start.

BRONWYN: And is that why you want to write a book about me? Out of gratitude? That isn't a good place to begin.

EDWARD: I would like to write an authorised account of your life.

Silence.

BRONWYN: Do you think you're the first person to darken my doorstep with such a request?

EMILY enters with a bottle of whisky from duty free.

EMILY: How are you two getting along?

BRONWYN: Famously.

She opens the bottle and pours herself a drink.

EMILY: *(To Edward.)* Wouldn't you like some whisky with that?

EDWARD: I'm alright, thanks.

EMILY: Mom?

BRONWYN: Thanks.

During the following, EMILY gives her mother a drink.

BRONWYN: Dr Smith wants to write my biography. Did you know that?

EMILY: *(Thrown for a moment.)* I had no idea. Did you agree to it?

BRONWYN: Who knows? It's unlikely I'll be here after tomorrow. Would it matter either way?

She drinks her whisky.

EMILY: You know Edward grew up in the same suburb as us?

BROWNYN: In Johannesburg?

EMILY: I mean in Highlands – Harare.

BROWNYN: You hardly grew up there, dear. We left Salisbury when you were five – or was it eight? *(To Edward.)* The war. My husband died at the height of it. After that I came down here and started to write.

EMILY: *(Ironic, to Edward.)* Maybe you should make a note of that for your book.

BROWNYN: I'm not going to say anything to Dr Smith that he won't find in a good archive of my work.

Silence.

EDWARD: And how long do you intend to stay in Johannesburg, Emily?

EMILY: Until my mother is back to her old self.

BROWNYN: Well you may have long to wait.

Silence.

BROWNYN: Emily is applying for a job.

EMILY: I'm only thinking about it.

EDWARD: Where?

EMILY: The English Department.

EDWARD: I didn't know they were advertising.

EMILY: You could apply for it.

EDWARD: Even if I wanted to –

EMILY: Don't worry about me. I've been quite comfortable in New York.

Silence.

BROWNYN: They'd be lucky to have her.

EDWARD: I'm sure they would.

BROWNYN: I'm pleased she's planning to return home.

EMILY: It hasn't quite come to that.

BROWNYN: Although I don't know what you're going to do about the children. What school are you intending to send them to? It isn't so easy to find a place at a good school in Johannesburg. There are waiting lists.

Silence.

EMILY: Mom, you're thinking about Jo. I don't have children.

BROWNYN: Of course. I knew that. *(To Edward.)* It's this –

She motions towards her head.

EMILY: I have an older sister called Jo who lives in Australia.

Silence.

BROWNYN: My grandchildren recently acquired Australian accents.

Silence.

EMILY: You could also note that down for your book.

Silence.

BROWNYN: Please excuse me. *(Standing up.)* I think I'll go and lie down. That whisky was probably a mistake.

EDWARD: *(Standing up.)* Of course.

BROWNYN: *(As she leaves.)* Emily, dear, I would like you to give Dr Smith access to the boxes in the garage.

EMILY: You mean – you're giving your approval to his book?

BROWNYN: I'm giving him the opportunity to say what he thinks. *(Waving her hand in his direction.)* Goodbye, Dr Smith.

EDWARD: Mrs Blackburne, I can't tell you how grateful I am –

BROWNYN: Then don't. We both know you're only doing this for yourself.

She leaves.

EDWARD: Did she really mean that?

EMILY: Believe me: if she said it, she meant it.

EDWARD: Then we have something to celebrate.

EMILY: We do?

Silence.

EMILY: Why didn't you tell me about your book?

EDWARD: Maybe the idea only just popped into my head.

EMILY: Somehow, I don't believe that.

She pours them each a shot. They clink glasses and drink.

EMILY: She only agreed because you're black.

EDWARD: Really?

EMILY: Look at her books. Black men have always been her blind spot.

EDWARD: And her daughter?

EMILY smiles, turns away.

EDWARD: I'll do her memory justice. I can promise you that.

EMILY: You're forgetting that she isn't actually dead yet.

Silence.

EMILY: And don't be fooled by those boxes in the garage. Those are only a ruse. You won't find anything new.

EDWARD: Are you implying your mother has something to hide?

EMILY: Not necessarily.

Silence.

EDWARD: Has anyone ever told you that you have her eyes?

EMILY: I was rather hoping I had my own eyes.

EDWARD: You do.

Silence.

EDWARD: It must have been hard – growing up under the shadow of a mother like that.

EMILY: Is that a question for me or your book?

EDWARD: For you, of course.

Silence.

EMILY: My mother has always surrounded herself with admirers. People who come between herself and her children. Why do you think my sister and me chose to live abroad? We didn't run away from South Africa. We ran away from her.

She extracts a key from behind a book.

EDWARD: What's that?

EMILY: Don't you recognise a key when you see one?

EDWARD: A key to what?

EMILY: *(Indicating the wooden chest.)* That chest.

EDWARD: And what's in that?

EMILY: All her old journals.

Silence.

EDWARD: Have you never opened it?

EMILY: Not since I was a child.

EDWARD: Do you think there's something in there? Something I should know about?

EMILY: I am doing what she asked for: giving you the opportunity to say what you think.

She steps forward and gives him the key.

EMILY: Didn't you say you came here for research?

EDWARD: But – why me?

EMILY: Because I have my mother's eyes. I have a blind spot when it comes to black men.

Silence.

EMILY: I've always liked that word 're-search'. The idea of searching for something again and again without the prospect of ever finding it.

He steps forward, kisses her.

EMILY: Haven't you seduced enough women for one night?

Edward kisses her again.

Blackout.

Part Two

BRONWYN's sitting room. A few weeks later. Late morning. EDWARD is looking through the contents of the wooden chest. He has a pile of notebooks and photograph albums already out and is deeply absorbed in reading something.

BRONWYN enters. She stands at the door and watches EDWARD. Her hair has been shaved off and she is wearing a simple dress. She looks smaller, diminished.

BROWNYN: Who asked you to do that?

EDWARD: *(Standing.)* Mrs Blackburne, I see you're back on the horse!

BROWNYN: The horse? What horse?

EDWARD: I mean you're up.

BROWNYN: Have we met?

EDWARD: I'm Edward.

BROWNYN: Are you here for an interview?

EDWARD: I'm your biographer.

BROWNYN: I have a biographer?

EDWARD: I'm writing a book about your life.

BROWNYN: And do you think you're up to that?

EDWARD: I hope so.

Silence.

BROWNYN: You don't look like you've read a book, let alone written one.

EDWARD: Oh yes?

BROWNYN: Let me look at your hands.

EDWARD: My hands?

He shows her his hands.

BROWNYN: A man with hands like that shouldn't write a book.

EDWARD: And why is that?

Silence.

EDWARD: Too soft, perhaps? Too black?

BROWNYN: Too ready for a fight.

She crosses to her chair and sits.

BROWNYN: Have we had breakfast yet?

EDWARD: It's almost time for lunch.

BROWNYN: I could eat a horse. Perhaps the one you were talking about. Did you see where it went?

EDWARD: No.

BROWNYN: Perhaps you could go and find it for me.

Silence.

BROWNYN: I'm only pulling your leg, Mr – ?

EDWARD: Dr – Edward Smith.

BROWNYN: Smith? And how did you come by the unlikely name of Smith?

EDWARD: That's a long story, Mrs Blackburne. I tend not to tell it.

During the following, he also sits. He has a notebook of his own and sometimes makes notes.

BROWNYN: Was I away for long?

EDWARD: You were in hospital for two weeks.

BROWNYN: I think I can remember that.

EDWARD: You were in a coma for several days. We thought for a while you wouldn't emerge. Emily was beside herself with worry. We both were. But then you fought your way back.

BROWNYN: And how long have I been at home?

EDWARD: Some weeks now.

Silence.

BROWNYN: And Emily?

EDWARD: She popped out to the shops. She made me promise to look after you.

BROWNYN: Really? And how will you do that?

EDWARD: *(Smiling.)* I have no idea. I find it hard enough to look after myself.

Silence.

BROWNYN: Well don't think I'm anything like Emily. I don't give myself away so easily.

Silence.

BROWNYN: People don't realise it about her at first. She comes across as an intellectual. Indifferent to her appearance. Altogether elsewhere. But men soon work out that she is a woman – lost. And they move in on that. Poor child. She leaves herself so defenceless that men simply walk in through the front door and start helping themselves – so to speak.

Silence.

BROWNYN: Are you in love with her?

EDWARD: Emily?

Silence.

BROWNYN: You say her name as if you've recently had sex with her. As if you now own a part of her. Don't worry – all men are the same. At least in the ways that matter.

Silence.

BROWNYN: It was always easier to love Jo. Not that I loved Emily less, you must understand, but with Emily it was more complicated. Jo was far away, like a little yacht at sea. Emily was too close for comfort. A life jacket I could never get off.

Silence.

BROWNYN: I hoped she'd have children. But I suppose it's getting a bit late for that. Do you think you might have made her pregnant?

EDWARD: Mrs Blackburne – I'm not sure this conversation is appropriate.

BROWNYN: I don't know why you're pretending to be polite. I can see at once that you can't be trusted. For some reason you've already turned against me. Was it something I said? Or was it something Emily said? I sometimes think Emily will only feel satisfied when I'm dead.

EDWARD: Why would you say that?

BROWNYN: Because I wasn't the mother she wanted. I was good enough for Jo, but never good enough for her.

EDWARD: Perhaps she thinks you chose writing before her?

BROWNYN: Is that what she said?

EDWARD: Not in so many words.

Silence.

BROWNYN: I'm not sure if it's possible to be a good mother and a good writer. And I'm not talking about someone who has managed to publish a couple of books. I'm talking about a real writer. The kind of writer who spends her whole life concentrated on little else but advancing her craft.

EDWARD: You're saying you have to choose?

BROWNYN: Every day. Whenever you close your door on your children.

Silence.

BROWNYN: Although for me it never felt like a choice. I was like a drug addict, you see, exercising great cunning to protect my habit.

EDWARD: At the expense of protecting your children?

BROWNYN: I never said that.

Silence.

EDWARD: There was something you once wrote. Can I read it to you?

BRONWYN shrugs.

EDWARD: *(Reading from her notebook.)* 'I had a very productive morning. Two thousand words, and half the day gone in a single glorious act of the imagination. I felt like a concert pianist at the typewriter – everything around me hushed. When I came around, my whole body still glowing, I remembered it was the school holidays. Felt immediate guilt and raced downstairs. I heard laughter and found Emily in the lounge talking to – X. Jo was playing tennis next door with Rebecca.' Do you remember writing that?

BROWNYN: No. Who is X?

EDWARD: You didn't write X. The name has been scribbled out. Do you have any idea why the name is scribbled out?

BROWNYN: No idea.

EDWARD: Then you carry on: 'There was something about the scene in the lounge that struck me as odd. Emily was standing in front of 'X', who was sitting on the couch, his hand on her shoulder, leaning towards her as if he had just whispered something in her ear. She was standing – shy, awkward, the way children do when they have to listen to two adults talking on the street and want to carry on walking. X stood abruptly when he saw me, said I'd given him a fright. I asked what they were talking about. He said nothing. He was telling her a story. I had a terrible feeling suddenly – that I had handed Emily over to something monstrous. I felt what the parents of sacrificed children must have felt. But of course this is absurd. I was no doubt infected by what I was writing, and thinking not so much of my own children as the children I was describing – starving in the Eastern Cape during the frontier wars.' No doubt? Was there really 'no doubt'?

BROWNYN: What are you trying to imply, Mr Smith?

EDWARD: I'm wondering what happened in the lounge. I'm wondering who this 'X' is. And I'm wondering why his name was scribbled out.

BROWNYN: He was a poet. A black consciousness poet who was staying for a few weeks in our house.

EDWARD: And you trusted this man?

BROWNYN: Why would I not? He was a good man. He wrote like an angel. In fact, his writing was honoured recently by our new government.

EDWARD: Then why did you remove his name?

BROWNYN: I don't recall doing so. But I suppose I wanted to protect him. I must have looked over that passage one day and decided I didn't want his name associated with – an aspersion like that.

EDWARD: An aspersion? You used the word 'monstrous'. That's quite an aspersion.

BROWNYN: As I say, I scribbled the name out.

EDWARD: I thought you said you didn't.

BROWNYN: Well – who could have if it wasn't me?

Silence.

EDWARD: I'm interested by this word 'monstrous'. You wrote a bit later in the same notebook a single sentence. 'I often fear that most great artists are in some way monstrous.' Were you talking about yourself or someone else?

BROWNYN: Perhaps I was writing down an idea for a book. Perhaps the whole event you just read out to me is no more than an idea for a book. Have you considered that? I would often do that. Experiment with different voices, different attitudes. Write down possible scenarios. There are literally hundreds of such notebooks around the place. How do you know that the incident I described even took place in the outside world?

EDWARD: Because it doesn't read like that.

BROWNYN: Well, I have no memory of it. For me it never took place.

Silence.

EDWARD: But why would you think of artists as monstrous?

BROWNYN: I suppose I was talking about the need for a fundamental selfishness. The way you're required to put your internal world – the dictates of your internal world – first.

EDWARD: And if necessary hand your own children over as some kind of sacrifice?

She sighs, impatient.

EDWARD: In psycho-analysis it's called an unholy exchange. Handing over something you want in order to get some other, more forbidden thing that at that moment you want more.

Silence.

EDWARD: When you were talking about Emily earlier, telling me how she gives herself away too easily – well it reminded me of that passage you wrote. It made me wonder: who handed whom over first?

Silence.

BROWNYN: This is ridiculous.

EDWARD: Did you ever ask Emily about this man – this poet?

BROWNYN: Not that I remember.

EDWARD: What if you were right? What if something unspeakable really was taking place in your sitting-room, while you were up there in your ivory tower, lost in your own imaginings?

BROWNYN: Every artist must feel that guilt. It doesn't mean I didn't love my children. Or that I failed to protect them.

EDWARD: Yet you didn't even try to get to the bottom of what was going on. Would you like me to read the next paragraph?

She shrugs.

EDWARD: 'As 'X' was about to leave, I told Emily to go next door and look for Jo. I made myself some coffee and went back upstairs. But the day was ruined. I couldn't get back into it. The will to return to where I had been flying so effortlessly moments before was gone.' Why do you think the will was gone? The day ruined? What happened between that man and your little girl, Mrs Blackburne? I think you know far more about all this than you're letting on.

BROWNYN: Get out!

EDWARD: I'm sorry?

BROWNYN: Get out of my house!

EDWARD stands.

EDWARD: Tell me something else: what book is worth one child's happiness?

BROWNYN: I never asked you to come in here.

EDWARD: I am your biographer. You gave me access to your private papers. You said I could say whatever I liked.

BROWNYN: Well I'm sure I never said you could make it up!

EDWARD: I'm a reader. That's what I do. I look very carefully at what people like you write – the so-called 'great' writers – and I form connections. That's my job. I'm sorry if it offends you.

BROWNYN: Where is Emily? Please – call her.

EDWARD: Emily is out buying the milk.

BROWNYN: Why do you want to torture us?

EDWARD: Torture? We're simply talking, Mrs Blackburne. Exchanging a few words. How can that be hurtful?

Silence.

EDWARD: There's a theory about writers – that at the heart of everything they write there's a single preoccupation. One they rework over and over again. Most of the time, they're unaware of it. If they became aware of it, they would probably have no need to write. The theory suggests that they only write in order to find out what it is they want to write about. The longer this takes, the more books they produce.

BROWNYN: Who are you, Mr Smith?

Silence.

EDWARD: You know what your preoccupation is? Guilt. The anatomy of guilt. I used to think it was the collective guilt of all your people. You were like a surgeon, cutting through the hypocrisy of the times with a carefully honed sentence. But it was your own guilt that you were trying to comprehend, wasn't it? All the rest – the politics of the time, any social injustices – those were just the trappings, the excuse, a way of making what you were doing seem more respectable.

Silence.

BROWNYN: I feel very tired. I think I would like to rest.

EDWARD: Of course.

BROWNYN: Will you let yourself out?

EDWARD: Eventually – yes.

Silence.

BROWNYN: I would like to ask you a favour, Mr Smith.

EDWARD: Dr Smith. Yes?

BROWNYN: Please leave me and my family alone.

EDWARD: I'm sorry. It's too late for that: I've opened your wooden chest. Do you want to know who gave me the key?

Silence.

EDWARD: I am in love with Emily. I want to marry her.

BROWNYN: You can marry Emily if you have to, but then you must forget about your book.

EDWARD laughs.

EDWARD: Are you trying to barter with me now, Mrs Blackburne?

BROWNYN: I only mean if you love each other. If it's what she wants to do. But your book. Putting words into people's mouths. Making them guilty of a thing you have only imagined. You know what that is? Nothing more than gossip.

EDWARD: That poet whose name you scribbled out. Is he still alive?

BROWNYN: He died in solitary confinement. He was tortured by the police. He was a very good man.

EDWARD: Was he really? A 'very good man'?

Silence.

EDWARD: I suppose we'll never know, will we? You never bothered to find out.

He walks out.

She doesn't move.

BROWNYN: Emily?

Silence.

BROWNYN: Emily?

The light fades to darkness.

Part Three

BRONWYN's sitting room. Later that day, around midnight. The room is dimly lit. There is an empty bottle of wine and two glasses.

EMILY and EDWARD are entwined on the couch, under a blanket.

EMILY: My first memory is of driving in convoy through the Rhodesian bush. I remember looking through the acacias, trying to spot a terrorist. It felt as if it was the same tree being repeated, again and again, but it wasn't the tree that was the same each time, it was the fear that stood behind it.

Silence.

EMILY: Later I learned to call terrorists freedom fighters, but the old word still sits somewhere behind the new word for me – like that fear behind every tree.

Silence.

EMILY: Did your father fight in the war?

EDWARD: My dad was a drunk. He spent most of his time lying inside the garden shed on an old couch. I once saw a spider crawling right over his mouth and he didn't even twitch.

EMILY: My father was a pilot. I remember having lunch one day at the Victoria Falls Hotel with a pilot friend of his. We sat outside, listening to that song "In the Jungle", and I made an elaborate sculpture out of straws of a giraffe. Everyone admired it. Later that afternoon we all drove to the airport. My father's friend was flying one Viscount back to Salisbury and we were flying in the other. I wanted to be in my father's friend's plane because it had curtains in the windows. A week later as he was flying out of Kariba, he and his plane were shot down by a group of guerrillas. The survivors – some of them babies and children – were bayonetted and shot. Unspeakable things were done to their bodies.

EDWARD: Why are you telling me this?

EMILY: In half a life, look how far we've come. I wonder what my father would have said if he could see us now.

EDWARD: It's interesting that the death of your father should have given your mother the freedom to write. And that your mother should write from the exact opposite perspective from the one she'd grown up with. Did your father die in the war?

EMILY: Apparently, he became delusional, paranoid. My mother told me he injected himself with morphine not long after that Viscount was shot down. But she never talks about it.

EDWARD: Another thing she doesn't like to talk about.

EMILY: What do you mean? What else is there?

He kisses her.

EMILY: Ouch.

EDWARD: What?

EMILY: You're scratching me.

EDWARD: Sorry, it's this damn belt.

He manages to remove his trousers.

They kiss.

EDWARD: At the conference – when did you know we'd have sex?

EMILY: As soon as you asked your question. And you?

EDWARD: As soon as I saw you sitting up there at the podium.

EMILY: What was it that attracted you?

EDWARD: The way you carried yourself. So upright. The way you tossed your hair back over your shoulder, like an afterthought. You were someone who didn't seem to pay much attention to the past. You were only interested in moving on.

EMILY: You're a strange man.

EDWARD: You don't know the half of it.

He removes some of her clothing during the following.

EMILY: The odd thing is, I remember my father's friend at lunch that day, but not my father. Where my father is meant to be, there's only a blank space. Perhaps he wasn't even there in the first place.

EDWARD: You have no other memories of him?

EMILY: Several images, but I might have got those from photographs. I clearly remember standing on his feet as he walked along the corridor of our house – towards the light of the front stoep. He was moaning like some sea monster while I was laughing. But even that I might have dreamed. Who knows what happened and what didn't, right?

EDWARD: Did anyone ever tell you that you talk too much?

Silence.

They are about to make love.

EDWARD: Are you with me, Emily?

EMILY: What?

EDWARD: Are you here with me?

EMILY: Where else would I be?

They stop moving.

EMILY: You can carry on.

EDWARD: Are you sure?

EMILY: Of course. Carry on.

He carries on.

Silence.

He stops.

EDWARD: I'm sorry.

He moves away from her.

EDWARD: I can't.

Silence.

EMILY: What's wrong?

EDWARD: I don't want to 'carry on'.

Silence.

EMILY: Perhaps you've had too much wine.

Silence.

EMILY: You drank most of the bottle.

Silence.

EMILY: Maybe we could just talk.

They lie there.

EMILY: What would you like to talk about?

EDWARD: I'm sorry.

He gets up, puts on his trousers, picks up the bottle, sees it's empty.

EDWARD: I feel like my father.

EMILY: How so?

EDWARD: He was always looking at the bottom of bottles he'd just drunk.

EMILY: Well, you at least have something to celebrate.

EDWARD: I do?

EMILY: Today you got my job.

Silence.

EDWARD: We both know you were the better candidate.

EMILY: That isn't true.

EDWARD: I was simply the darker candidate.

Silence.

EDWARD: Why aren't you more pissed off about it?

EMILY: Who would you like me to be pissed off with? You? The panel? The country? Cecil Rhodes?

EDWARD: You're so damn passive.

EMILY: I am?

EDWARD pours himself some whisky. He downs it.

EMILY: Whenever we have sex, why do you always have to be drunk?

Silence.

EMILY: *(Pulling on some clothes.)* What happened today?

EDWARD: What are you talking about?

EMILY: When I got home, you were in the garage and my mother was lying in my bed, holding onto my pillow. It looked like she'd been crying. And neither of you wanted to talk.

EDWARD: Nothing happened. I was just – preoccupied.

Silence.

EDWARD: Do you think she'll recover?

EMILY: This afternoon in the bath she was talking in a language I couldn't understand. There was some French in it, some German and Spanish. She sounded like Finnegan's Wake.

EDWARD: She still has a fundamentally European head. Which is quite an accomplishment these days, don't you think?

EMILY: What's wrong, Edward?

Silence.

EDWARD: Are you secretly wishing she was dead?

EMILY: Why would you say such a thing?

EDWARD: Well you seem to hate her so much.

EMILY: What gives you that idea?

EDWARD: Why else did you give me that key?

EMILY: The key to the chest? Why not? I didn't actually think she has anything to hide. Perhaps a love letter from a married man or two – but nothing else.

EDWARD: Is that really what you thought?

Silence.

EMILY: What did you find?

EDWARD: Today we talked about a poet. Someone who was killed in detention. Do you remember him staying in this house? *(Sarcastic.)* Like me – he was black.

EMILY: We've always had lots of writers coming and going around here.

EDWARD: Apparently the two of you liked to talk in this room. He used to sit on that couch. He used to make you laugh. Do you remember what you laughed about?

EMILY: Why is this so important?

EDWARD: Maybe it is, maybe it isn't. Maybe it's killed everything.

EMILY: You aren't making any sense.

EDWARD: Have you read those notebooks before? Did you want me to find the passages about him? Was it you who scratched out his name?

EMILY: I have never read those books in my life. As a girl I might have – but I could never read her writing. Even now I find it difficult. What do you mean – scratched out his name?

EDWARD: Maybe you saw that man's name written there and you hated it so much, or feared it so much, that you wanted to scribble it out.

EMILY: What are you trying to tell me, Edward? That something took place between me and that man?

EDWARD: Your mother suspects it.

He goes over to the chest and takes out the top notebook. He tosses it in her lap and switches on a lamp.

EDWARD: The page is marked. Read it.

She opens the book, looks at it.

EMILY: What am I looking at?

EDWARD: God knows. An idea for a novel, perhaps. Or perhaps it's the moment your mother destroyed your life.

EMILY: *(Looking at the passage.)* I have no memory of – any of this.

EDWARD: That's what she said.

EMILY: Aren't all parents the same? Suspecting every adult who shows too much interest in their child? It doesn't mean anything happened.

EDWARD: It doesn't mean it didn't.

Silence.

EMILY: If I was interfered with in some way, surely I'd remember it.

EDWARD: Yes, I imagine you would.

EMILY: Yet – I don't.

Silence.

EDWARD: These things can be repressed.

Silence.

EDWARD: Tell me, Emily. What do you see in me?

EMILY: Right now, a lot of drink.

EDWARD: Why did you give yourself over to me so easily?

EMILY: At the conference? I liked the question you asked about my mother. I thought it was intelligent.

EDWARD: And you like intelligent black men? Like your mother?

EMILY: Edward – let's not say anything we might regret.

Silence.

EDWARD: It was all too easy. To seduce you. At first I couldn't believe my luck. Until today I even thought that it might have been love, or the start of something like love. But do you know what you just did to me? You made me feel – dirty. Even though you weren't actually enjoying it, you wanted me to carry on. Why? Why would you do that to yourself?

EMILY: I suppose I'm still feeling pissed off about the job.

EDWARD: But you told me you didn't want it. You encouraged me to apply for it!

EMILY: What did you expect me to say? 'That's my job – not yours – and I got there first'?

Silence.

EDWARD: But you have a whole life in New York. You said you don't even want to live in this country.

EMILY: Well, as it happens I can only work in the department as long as I'm doing my PhD. And I handed my thesis in last month.

Silence.

EMILY: All my belongings are in boxes at a friend's apartment, ready to be shipped back. At the moment, this house is the closest I have to a home.

EDWARD: Why didn't you tell me that?

EMILY: Because maybe I didn't want to seem too desperate.

Silence.

EDWARD: *(Coming closer to her.)* Listen, Emily. I think we need to talk.

EMILY: About what?

EDWARD: About my book.

EMILY: Really? That's about all we ever talk about. Can't we talk about something else?

EDWARD: I'm afraid it's going to take a different course.

EMILY: *(Ironic.)* What – have you decided to write a novel instead?

EDWARD: And I'll need your support. Because your mother isn't going to like it.

Silence.

EMILY: You are asking me to gang up on my mother– is that it?

EDWARD: It will take courage from you. To stand up at last and speak the truth.

EMILY: What on earth are you talking about?

EDWARD: Admit it, Emily – you're fucked up. You have a reputation for sleeping around. God – even your mother says so.

Silence.

EDWARD: But I want to help you. I want us to get to the truth.

EMILY: So you can write about it – and sell lots of books?

EDWARD: No, I love you. I want to reach you – and make everything alright.

EMILY: Tell me something, when did you decide you wanted to write this book? When you asked me that question at the conference or before that? Did you come to the conference in the first place because you knew I'd be there? Did you think you'd come and seduce me first?

EDWARD: That isn't how it happened.

EMILY: I think that's exactly how it happened.

Silence.

EMILY: I've been watching you. You barely miss a Silence.

EDWARD: What's that supposed to mean?

EMILY: Underneath your great torrent of words, you have a blank look. Like you're already half dead. Have you ever actually meant anything you've said?

EDWARD: I have only ever tried to get to the truth.

EMILY: You go around using words like 'love' and 'truth'. But when you say those words, I find myself wanting to laugh. It's becoming clearer and clearer to me that you wouldn't recognise love or truth if they were staring you in the face.

Silence.

EDWARD: I know that your mother handed you over to the world before you were ready. I know she gave you up so she could write. And while the rest of the world was holding her up as this model of virtue, this great champion of free speech, she was busy suppressing the truth about what she'd allowed in her own house. Don't you think it's time someone exposed that? She's only ever served herself – and you, Emily, you were the sacrifice!

EMILY: All of this from a few lines in a notebook?

EDWARD: Her discomfort with herself is inside every book she ever wrote. I have always wondered about the source of it.

EMILY: That was your question, wasn't it? 'Why do you think your mother's books are always so preoccupied with the anatomy of guilt?'

EDWARD: And even then you refused to answer it. Why did you refuse to answer it?

EMILY: Because I don't like to speak about my mother in public.

EDWARD: So much for free speech!

EMILY: There's a difference between free speech and speaking too freely, Edward.

EDWARD: That depends on what it is you're trying to protect.

Silence.

EDWARD: I thought your mother was different. I thought, 'Here is a woman who has spent her whole life writing about something wider, deeper, more complex than herself and her own interests. She has written her way into lives and places like no other white African writer has ever done before.' But when I came here and entered her house, all I saw was racks of silver, oil paintings, Persian rugs – and a stoep with its view over the conquered land. And I wondered, 'Who is this woman really?' She sits up there in her sacred tower, where no one else is ever allowed to set foot, and comes up with this idea of herself. As the hero of the people. Yet she never gets her hands dirty. She's up there paring her bloody fingernails, while her little girl is downstairs in this very room being –

EMILY Being what? Can you even say it?

EDWARD: Raped.

Silence.

EDWARD: By a black man without a face.

Silence.

EMILY: I promise you, Edward – if you write anything about any of this, I will never speak to you again.

EDWARD: Are you also trying to censor me?

EMILY: I'm trying to stop you from making a terrible mistake.

EDWARD: I'm not the one around here making terrible mistakes.

EMILY: It's nothing more than defamation.

EDWARD: The proof is somewhere. And I intend to find it.

EMILY: You sound like a madman, do you know that?

EDWARD: Is that why you were drawn to me? Was I another black man without a face? Is that what you want – to re-enact your experience of abuse? You're probably getting off on this – getting used and abused all over again.

EMILY: That is a horrible thing to say.

EDWARD: Is it? Look into your body. Look into your sex. The answer is there, waiting for you. Why do you throw yourself at men? Why do you give yourself away so easily? Because your mother as good as gave you away as a child. And why? Simply so she could write a book!

EMILY: Edward, if you write about any of this anywhere, we will be at war. Do you understand me?

EDWARD: Then war it is.

Blackout.

Part Four

Several months later. Late afternoon. Winter. BRONWYN's sitting room. A clock ticks. There are notebooks strewn all over the floor, the couch. A fire glows.

EMILY enters. She is visibly pregnant and looks radiant with health. She starts to gather up the notebooks from the wooden chest – then stops, sits, opens one.

She starts to read:

EMILY: 'Emily's questions fill me with wonder: "Mummy, where does the sea come from?" "How do you reach your hand to move it?" "What do trees do when they get a sore knee?" She thinks blood is in the objects around her, not her own body. And that when you fall the blood comes out the objects and lands on your body and hurts you. She will say: "Mummy, does that pavement have blood in it?" '

BRONWYN enters, wearing an old dressing-gown and a woollen hat. She looks pale, sick, lost.

BROWNYN: I heard voices downstairs. Do we have guests?

EMILY: No, today it's just us.

BROWNYN: And the children. *(She looks around at the invisible children.)* It takes half the day to get them ready to go out. What they will wear and what they won't. This one doesn't want to wear those shoes because they make her trip, that one doesn't want those socks because they make his feet itch. *(Smiling tenderly at one of them.)* Thomas had a temperature all night. I wanted to run him a cool bath, but I couldn't move my legs. Luckily this morning he took all his medicine and is feeling much better. It tastes horrible, but I follow it up with a teaspoon of sugar and we wash it down with a glass of water. If he can keep it all down without gagging, he gets a white marshmallow at the end of it. He draws the line at pink.

EMILY: I'm glad he's feeling better.

BROWNYN: Who?

EMILY: Thomas.

BRONWYN looks around, as if suddenly the children have disappeared. But she is happy to find them there again. During the following, she wanders around – she never quite settles.

EMILY: I've been reading your journals. The ones from the chest. I thought they'd be all about your writing, and literature, but you know what you write about mainly? Me and Jo. Everything we've said and done from the moment we were born. I've spent the whole day weeping.

BRONWYN looks at her blankly.

EMILY: You were good mother, Mom. You still are.

BROWNYN: They keep me busy. All those mouths to feed.

Silence.

EMILY: Who was Henry?

BROWNYN: Henry?

EMILY: You write a lot about him too. Especially in your early journals.

BROWNYN: He was my husband.

EMILY: No, your husband was called Tom. Thomas Blackburne. My father.

BROWNYN: Of course.

EMILY: And Henry?

BROWNYN: Like a bird on fire. He fell from the sky.

Silence.

BROWNYN: And I loved him.

EMILY: I see.

She picks up another journal, pages through it.

EMILY: You wrote this when we were already in
Johannesburg: 'Today I sat at my desk all day and thought
about Henry. I want nothing more than to write about him.
He is the only thing I want to write about. But of course it's
impossible.'

BROWNYN: Did you write that?

EMILY: You did.

BROWNYN: What else did I write?

EMILY: 'I wish I could go back to that moment. Standing
on that little pathway that wound through the forest, the
children having run on ahead. He stopped me and pulled
me into a long, deep kiss, like he was gasping for breath.
Our faces were wet with the mist. The water roared in our
ears, made it almost impossible to speak. And that was the
last time we touched.'

Silence.

EMILY: Was that at the Victoria Falls Hotel?

BROWNYN: It was our final kiss.

EMILY: And that man we had lunch with? Was he Dad's friend?
Was that Henry?

Silence.

BROWNYN: He died because he loved me.

EMILY: He came to the hotel to be with you, didn't he?

BROWNYN: Did he? To be with me?

EMILY: I think you and Henry spent the weekend together.
I think you were going to leave Dad. Is that what you'd
decided?

BROWNYN: We decided when we kissed.

EMILY: And then he was shot down. Like a bird on fire. Is that how it happened, Mom?

BROWNYN: I do remember that kiss.

EMILY: I remember his airplane. His had curtains, ours did not. Somewhere else you wrote: 'Emily cried as we walked towards our plane. I don't know why she was crying. But I could see she knew that I loved him. And I could see that made her want to love him too. Henry made us laugh. He made the world feel lighter, less stuck. Thomas was always brooding, jealous, the air around him full of thunder.'

Silence.

EMILY: Did Daddy know about your affair?

Silence.

BROWNYN: He didn't say anything. I thought he would hit me, but he walked out.

EMILY: Did you know he planned to kill himself?

BROWNYN: We hardly spoke after that.

EMILY: *(Reading again.)* 'Morphine. From Morpheus, the god of sleep. He had the syringes and enough morphine for each of us. He came and told me that. He said we would lose the war. That it was just a matter of time before we'd all be slaughtered in our beds. He said it would be easier if we went to sleep now. While still together, as a family. I said I had ordered the girls a chocolate cake for tea. I asked if he would go and pick it up for us – from Helen's Cakes, at the Highlands shops. Then I packed one suitcase for all of us. And herded the girls into the car. I was just starting the engine when he came back. He parked right up behind me, making it impossible to get out. I saw him open the door, balancing the cake, a question on his face. So I just drove off through the rose garden, the car screeching through the bushes, and bumped away across the grass. I didn't stop until I'd reached Johannesburg.

The girls complaining all the way, the car like an oven, smelling of hot plastic, and Thomas lying dead in the bed my parents gave us.'

Silence.

EMILY: And you never called the police?

BROWNYN: I never said a word about it. Not to anyone.

Silence.

EMILY: Mom – did you want Daddy to die?

Silence.

EMILY: Later you wrote: 'Now that he's gone, at last I have some space to think.'

She closes the book, looks at her mother. She moves away.

   Silence.

EMILY: Do you remember Edward?

Silence.

EMILY: I'm having his child.

BROWNYN: Is he ready for that?

EMILY: Edward?

BROWNYN: He's still a child himself.

Silence.

BROWNYN: Of all the children, Edward is the most afraid of doctors. When he last got sick, he said, 'Can't I just get better by myself?'

EMILY: Edward is writing a book about your life.

BROWNYN: I didn't want an argument. So I said to him, 'Don't worry. The body is very good at fixing itself. Especially with children. They heal so easily.'

EMILY: They do?

Silence.

EMILY: Did I heal easily?

BROWNYN: You were good at avoiding injuries. Not like
    Edward, who was always being stung by bees or wasps,
    falling off the garden wall into the hydrangeas. He put his
    finger in an electric socket three times, but somehow he
    always managed to survive it.

EMILY: I think you're talking about Jo. Edward is a biographer
    – and a father.

BROWNYN: *(Looking at her belly.)* The father of our new child?

EMILY: Yes.

BROWNYN: What will we call him?

EMILY: It's too early to tell.

BROWNYN: It's about time I had another son. This time, you'll
    see – I'll do a better job of it. I want him to smile more
    easily, love more fiercely. I can already see him playing
    airplanes in the park, flying over enemy lands without
    a thought. He'll grow tall, and I'll love every bit of him.
    I won't let him spill a single drop of blood. If he does, I
    will lick it up, like one of those women out of Lorca. And
    on my last day, when the darkness comes drifting in like
    smoke, the thought of him will be my sun.

EMILY: He'll be my son, Mom. Not yours.

Silence.

EMILY: *(Softening.)* But if you like, sometimes you can borrow
    him.

Silence.

BROWNYN: And the father? Is he somewhere here in the house?

EMILY: The father, I'm afraid, came to an ignominious end.

BROWNYN: He was always accident prone. Did he die?

EMILY: I haven't spoken to him in a long time. He may as well be dead.

BROWNYN: Well I did the best I could with each of them.

EMILY: Did you?

BROWNYN: With so many children, it's difficult to keep track. They're always running in and out the room, trying to talk at once. I find it impossible to listen to more than one voice at a time.

EMILY: You only have two children, Mom.

BROWNYN: Me? No, I have hundreds of children. Far too many heads to count.

Silence.

EMILY: What about poets? Did you ever have too many poets in this house?

BROWNYN: There were always too many poets in this house.

EMILY: And did you have a fight with any of them?

BROWNYN: Probably. They're a difficult lot.

EMILY: Was there one in particular who disappointed you?

BROWNYN: Not that I remember.

Silence.

BROWNYN: Why do you ask?

EMILY: It doesn't matter.

Silence.

EMILY: There are so many versions of a person. How do we know which one to hold on to and which one to relinquish?

BROWNYN: It's always important to know what to edit out.

Silence.

EMILY: I heard you typing again last night. Were you writing something new?

BROWNYN: I was trying to get to the end of the sentence.

EMILY: I think you've earned the right to rest.

BROWNYN: But I've hardly started.

EMILY: You've written almost thirty books, Mom. They are read and admired all over the world.

BROWNYN: I'm afraid you're thinking of someone else.

Silence.

BROWNYN: I should be getting on. A small boy is walking away from me. I must catch up with him before he slips off.

EMILY: Alright, Mom. You go ahead. I'll put the supper on.

BRONWYN stands and shuffles out the room. She waits so some of the children can pass through the door ahead of her, and then she goes.

EMILY sits very still, her hands around her belly, as the light fades to darkness.

Part Five

BRONWYN's sitting room. A few months later. Morning. Spring. BRONWYN is sitting at a desk, in the gloom, typing. She is wearing her pyjamas and an old coat.

EMILY enters, looking slim, pale, her hair loose. She opens the curtains to reveal a dappled Spring morning. Thrushes sing in the trees. She sighs wearily – and starts to tidy up during the following.

EMILY: You're up early.

> *There is no response from BRONWYN. She will type, now and again, during the scene, between long pauses.*

EMILY: Today I thought we could take a drive. Perhaps to the lion park. I haven't been there since I was a child. Do you remember the one in Rhodesia? You had a story about it.

> *Silence.*

EMILY: Otherwise we could go to the Home of the Chicken Pie. They had rabbits once. We used to push bits of cabbage for them through the wire mesh, but the goats usually got there first. You used to take me and Jo. I was good it imitating the peacock. It sounded like a baby cry.

> *Silence.*

EMILY: Are you writing another book?

> *BRONWYN looks at the typewriter. She pulls out a piece of paper. EMILY takes it, reads.*

EMILY: A new story? I hope it has a happier ending. You were never much good at those. You used to say, 'We haven't earned a happy ending yet.' You also used to say: 'Emily, we aren't important enough for tragedy.'

> *BRONWYN stares at her blankly.*

EMILY: I never knew if you were talking about the family or the country generally. Perhaps you didn't like to distinguish. You were never really our mother. You always belonged to something more important.

BRONWYN sneezes.

EMILY: I never wanted to be a mother as a result. Until recently, of course. Then I wanted it more than I'd ever wanted anything. Which was a mistake, naturally.

BRONWYN resumes typing.

EMILY: When we were scared of going to a children's birthday party, or jumping off a diving board, you liked to tell us about Aristotle. Courage is the mid-point between cowardice and foolhardiness, you'd say. Yes – you were always about the in-between spaces. Which is great philosophically, but it's not what children want. They want clear lines to cross or not to cross. The illusion of order while they're growing up. So they can feel they've grown up straight, and are able to think straight, and can go out and aim for what they want. We were always made to think about what was outside of ourselves first – and always felt outside of ourselves as a result. Don't be selfish, you'd say. As if that was the worst crime of all. To claim something for yourself. To stand for a few moments in the light.

There is a buzz at the front door. EMILY leaves the room. BRONWYN puts in fresh paper and stares at her machine. We hear voices.

EMILY and EDWARD enter.

EMILY: I didn't think you'd come.

EDWARD: I didn't think you'd ask.

EMILY: Because of your book?

EDWARD: You mean you read it?

EMILY: I paged through it in a bookshop. I read enough.

EDWARD: And yet you still invited me in here?

EMILY: Your book is not nearly as significant as you think.

EDWARD: No one wants to buy it. I suppose it's out of loyalty to your –

BRONWYN types. EDWARD sees her.

EDWARD: Mrs Blackburne, I'm sorry, I –

BRONWYN doesn't look up. She stares at the page and then types a letter or two.

EMILY: She doesn't speak.

Silence.

EMILY: I sometimes think she can understand me, at other times she seems completely blank. Like a page without any writing on it.

EDWARD: I had no idea.

Silence.

EDWARD: And you are looking after her?

EMILY: There's a woman called Makhosi who comes during the week. But at the weekends it's generally just the two of us.

Silence.

EMILY: Today we were thinking of going on an outing. Perhaps to the Lion Park.

EDWARD: She likes that?

EMILY: I've taken her to the zoo a few times. The sight of wild animals seems to perk her up.

Silence.

EMILY: When I was only a few months old, she and my father visited a lion park somewhere in Rhodesia. I was asleep in my car chair at the back, and they were watching a pride of lions sleeping under a tree. Then I woke up and let out a cry, and they said there were suddenly two lions' faces at the car window. They didn't even see the lions move. One moment the lions were asleep, the next they were there.

Silence.

EMILY: Fortunately for me, my mother had closed all the windows.

EDWARD: Why are you telling me this?

EMILY: Does every story have to have a reason?

EDWARD: Yes.

Silence.

EMILY: Well – maybe you were wrong about my mother. In your book. Maybe she knew when to open and when to close the windows.

Silence.

EMILY: And the door to our house.

EDWARD: I wish I could believe that.

EMILY: I did get around to reading her journals, by the way. Why didn't you tell me that they were full of things about me – me and my sister? And why didn't you mention them in your book?

EDWARD: All that obsessive recording she did, it was only so she could use you for some novel she planned to write. She wanted all the authentic details written down before she forgot.

EMILY: And yet she never did use those details in any of her books, did she? She published nearly thirty novels, but only rarely did a detail from those journals find its way into any one of them.

Silence.

EMILY: Perhaps the problem with your book is the problem with most criticism. The source material never quite manages to fit into the argument.

EDWARD: *(Looking at Bronwyn.)* Are you sure she can't understand us?

EMILY: She left this room long ago.

Silence.

He moves away.

EDWARD: What are your plans?

EMILY: I've applied for a job at a university in Perth.

EDWARD: Really? And you're still prepared to risk telling me about a vacancy?

EMILY: Oh, I wouldn't tell you if the application deadline hadn't already passed.

They smile.

EDWARD: And your mother?

EMILY: If she's still here, I'll take her with me.

EDWARD: You think she'd be able to leave this house?

EMILY: She was never very sentimental about property. And these days she doesn't even know her own name. She usually thinks I'm the nurse.

EDWARD: But the previous Bronwyn – she wouldn't like the idea of it.

Silence.

EMILY: Well, I might have stayed. If the university had given me that job.

Silence.

EMILY: I want to be near my sister and her children. Is that so terrible?

EDWARD: And will you ever come back to South Africa?

EMILY: Perhaps now and again – for research.

EDWARD: In order to look for something that might not exist?

Silence.

EMILY: And you, Edward?

Silence.

EMILY: Have you been enjoying my job?

EDWARD: You know me. I've never been much good at happiness.

EMILY: Actually, I didn't know that about you.

Silence.

EMILY: Would you like something to drink?

EDWARD: Water, thanks.

EMILY: Alright.

She leaves. He stands there, glances across at BRONWYN. She stares at him. He tries to smile. He waves. She simply looks back at him, with no change in her expression.

EMILY enters with two glasses of water.

EDWARD: When my book came out, I felt depressed.

She hands him a glass of water. He drinks all of it.

EMILY: It didn't exactly go down well with the critics. In fact, I've yet to meet one of my mother's old acquaintances who admits to having read it. If they have a copy, they're probably keeping it hidden under a cushion somewhere. Like they used to do with pornography.

EDWARD: Is it as bad as that?

EMILY: Why do you think you felt so depressed afterwards? Because you'd underestimated my mother – or because you'd underestimated yourself?

Silence.

EDWARD: I never actually betrayed your trust.

EMILY: All you said was that something terrible had been done to me as a child because of my mother's neglect. You mention a prominent poet – and withhold his name as if you know it but out of some ethical compunction have decided not to disclose it. Your argument is that my mother was cold, hard, a narcissist – yet you ignore those hundreds of journals that are about little more than her children, and her friends, and all the things in the world she loved.

Silence.

EDWARD: Maybe you don't remember what happened to you, but who's to say it didn't happen?

EMILY: Because I would feel it somewhere in my body. Those were your words, and I think they're accurate. Which also makes me wonder – how is it you can be so accurate? And how is it that you allowed that idea – which was little more than a rumour – to ruin not only your book but your career, your life?

EDWARD: What are you saying?

EMILY: Was it your father? Did he hurt you when he was drunk?

EDWARD: I see where this is going.

EMILY: We've had sex, Edward. I know you can only get aroused when you're drunk. I have felt parts of you that perhaps no one else has experienced, and I have glimpsed them time and again, like hideous phantoms, peering from behind every paragraph of your book.

EDWARD: I thought you only paged through it in a bookshop.

EMILY: I might have read some sections more carefully than others.

Silence.

EDWARD: So this is why you asked me here? To hear my confession?

Silence.

EDWARD: You want me to tell you I was raped, is that it? While my father was lying drunk in his garden hut, I was up in the house, with the big white boss, being abused? Is that the sordid little story you want me to trot out?

EMILY: I don't know, Edward – is it?

EDWARD: Naturally that's why I hate white people. I'm walking around with this big ungovernable wound. And that is why I'm incapable of governing myself – and writing a level-headed, sensible book. And perhaps that's why no black man will ever be capable of governing anything – because we're all too emotional, too angry, too wounded by the past ever to be sensible about anything again?

EMILY: I never said – any of that.

EDWARD: You don't need to. I know how you people think.

Silence.

EDWARD: Well I can tell you now: you aren't going to get my story, or get off on my story. I'm not ready to spill my guts all over this floor for your entertainment. My people have given enough. And I'm not going to make myself acceptable, digestible, comprehensible to you!

EMILY: Then why are you so upset? If there's no truth in what I'm saying, why does what I say make you so passionate?

EDWARD: I am not answerable to you.

Silence.

EMILY: You know why I asked you to come here? Because I liked you before. I wanted to find a reason to like you again.

EDWARD: So you dredged up an explanation for my bad behaviour? My bitterness? People are not so simple.

EMILY: Perhaps you should have told yourself that when you tried to represent my mother's life.

Silence.

EMILY: How does it feel – having your own methods turned back on you?

EDWARD: *(Losing it suddenly.)* What are you trying to do to me!

Silence.

EDWARD: I have to leave.

He heads towards the door.

EMILY: I was pregnant.

He stops.

EMILY: With your child.

Silence.

EDWARD: Where – is it?

EMILY: Gone.

EDWARD: You killed it?

EMILY: I lost it.

Silence.

EMILY: I miscarried after six months.

Silence.

EMILY: He was a boy. I saw him, and he was perfect. The only thing he lacked was a life.

EDWARD: And he – he was ours?

EMILY: He was. He was almost ours. But the spark inside him floated off. In the end, we weren't the right – starting place.

EDWARD stands there, completely bereft, trying to breathe.

During the following, he sits, his head in his hands, trying to contain his grief.

BROWNYN: 'Once upon a time, there was an old woman who sat in the top of a tall house that overlooked a difficult city. She told stories to herself, but she intended them for other people. Her stories were translated into many languages and her books migrated all over the world. One of these books landed in the lap of a young man called Edward. He was from the old woman's country, but he was far from home. The young man read her stories and decided to change his life. He continued to travel the world with the old woman's words flying around inside him, creating little pathways in his head that soon became his own.'

Silence.

EDWARD: I'm sorry.

Silence.

EDWARD: What should I do?

Silence.

EMILY: I don't know. But you could stay for supper, if you like.

Silence.

EMILY: We could talk. Or not talk. We could do whatever felt right.

EDWARD looks up at her.

EDWARD: Did it hurt?

EMILY: Yes.

Silence.

EMILY: And it hasn't stopped.

BROWNYN: 'One day, the young man met a woman. She was holding a glass of water. The young man stepped forward and took the glass, and he started to drink.'

EDWARD: Emily?

EMILY: Yes?

EDWARD: I'd like to tell it to you – my story. If you're still interested.

EMILY: Of course I am.

Silence.

EDWARD: It isn't easy.

EMILY: Who said it had to be?

They manage a smile.

BRONWYN starts typing again as the light fades to darkness.

The End.

Author Biography

Craig Higginson is an internationally acclaimed writer who lives in Johannesburg. His plays have been performed and produced at the National Theatre (London), the Royal Shakespeare Company, the Trafalgar Studios (London's West End), the Traverse Theatre (Edinburgh), the Stadsteater (Stockholm), Salisbury Theatre, the Citizens Theatre (Glasgow), Live Theatre (Newcastle), Next Theatre (Chicago), Theatre 503 and the Finborough Theatre (both London), the Market Theatre (Johannesburg) and several other theatres and festivals around the world. He was one of ten playwrights from around the world to be commissioned for his play *Little Foot* by the National Theatre (London) for the 2012 Connections Festival. He is currently adapting *The Mission Song* for John le Carre's production company The Ink Factory (London and LA) and for Headlong in the UK – for production in 2017. His new play *The Red Door* will also be produced and published in 2016.

Craig's awards in the UK and South Africa include the Sony Gold Award for the Best Radio Drama in the UK, an Edinburgh Fringe First, the UJ Award for South African Literature in English and Naledi Awards for Best South African play and Best Children's Play. His plays are published by Oberon Books and Methuen (London) and Wits Press (South Africa) and his novels by Picador Africa (Johannesburg) and Mercure de France (Paris).

His plays include: *Laughter in the Dark*, *Lord of the Flies*, *Truth in Translation* (co-writer), *Dream of the Dog*, *Ten Bush* (co-writer), *The Jungle Book*, *The Girl in the Yellow Dress*, *Little Foot* and *The Imagined Land*. His novels include: *The Hill*, *Last Summer*, *The Landscape Painter* and *The Dream House*, which was published in English in April 2015 – and will appear in 2016 in French. *Last Summer* will appear in French in 2017.

Craig was born in Zimbabwe and has lived in London, Stratford-upon-Avon, Paris and Johannesburg. He is married with one daughter.